# Moments in a Life

## Depression isn't all bad

### Rod Somerville

Second Edition

First published by Rodney Somerville 2021
Second Edition 2023

Copyright ©Rodney Somerville 2021

All rights reserved. Without limiting the rights under copyright reserved above, no part of this publication may be reproduced, stored in or introduced into a retrieval system, or transmitted, in any form or by any means (electronic, mechanical, photocopying, recording, or otherwise) without the prior written permission of the publishers of this book.

Moments in a Life: Depression isn't all Bad is educational material designed to inform and entertain.

Every care has been taken to trace and acknowledge copyright. Please let the author know of any accidental infringement and it will be addressed.

Typeset in Garamond by the publishers
Layout and design by Rod Somerville
Cover image by Rod Somerville

National Library of Australia
Cataloguing-in-Publication data

Creator: Somerville, Rodney, author

Title: Moments in a Life: Depression isn't all Bad / Rodney Somerville

ISBN: 978-0-6450987-4-7 (paperback)

Subjects: Autobiography, Mental Health, Depression, Uplifting Stories

**To all my family and friends.**

Without you my life would not have been nearly as interesting and wonderful.

# Contents

**PREFACE**
**PART ONE: CHRONOLOGY**
    Chapter One: Growing Up      13
    Chapter Two: Education      39
    Chapter Three: Working Life      51
**PART TWO: LIFE**
    Chapter Four: Injuries      87
    Chapter Five: Death      101
    Chapter Six: Sport      111
    Chapter Seven: Travelling      127
    Chapter Eight: The Natural World      205
    Chapter Nine: People With 'Interesting' Ideas      233
**PART THREE: PASSION**
    Chapter Ten: Astronomy      239
    Chapter Eleven: UFOs      275
**AFTERWORD**
**IMAGES**
**ABOUT THE AUTHOR**

# Preface

There is no getting around the fact that I am a nobody. In the grand scheme of the universe I have never done anything of earth-shattering importance or fame. However, that does not mean I haven't led an interesting life or had an influence on my own small sphere around me. Everybody has stories to tell and moments in their lives that are just as exciting and just as interesting as those among us with more widespread notoriety. In a lot of cases, more so.

There is also no getting around the fact that for half of my life I have lived with fluctuating levels of depression. Sometimes suicidal, sometimes just deeply sad, but always there since the age of 30. There seemed to be no end to the cycle of deep depressive episodes punctuated by the occasional brief period of almost not-unhappy times. During the low moments, I became quite good at hiding my feelings from everyone, always managing to smile and be cheerful on the outside, while inwardly wishing I could simply cease to exist, or that I had never been born. Occasionally things would slip and my inner torment would manifest itself, but these occasions were rare as I would try and avoid contact with other people when I knew I was in that frame of mind.

Then an unplanned moment occurred that helped me realise my life hasn't been so bad.

It may seem an odd thing to say, but when my mother died, I felt as happy and at peace as I had been for decades. Don't get me wrong, I loved my mother and am still sad she is no longer actively in my life, but towards the end, both she and I knew the time was coming and I knew how much pain and suffering she was experiencing. Once she finally passed away and my immediate sadness and grief subsided, I had an overwhelming feeling of happiness for her. The problems she suffered through in her final years were now over and she was at peace. Also, unlike with my father, I had the opportunity to say goodbye and come to terms with her own feelings about her impending death. Having the time to process all this while she was still alive meant that once it arrived I could more easily reflect on all the great moments I had with her throughout my life, and that brought me great joy and happiness.

Now, where am I heading with this?

I have also suffered for many decades with a weight problem (which didn't help with the depression). So, about a year after my mother died, I was feeling good enough about myself to visit my brother for a week on his farm to get some psychological help to try and lose some weight. He is a clinical psychologist and I thought he might be able to help.

His farm is nestled in the hills in the northeastern region of New South Wales. Located at the end of the road, 40 kilometres from the nearest town, it is a peaceful retreat, perfect for having some psychological therapy and feeling overwhelmingly relaxed. Of course, the therapy each day wouldn't last much more than an hour, so there was plenty of time to stop and while away the rest of the day talking over cups of tea and generally doing not much of anything. It was during these times that, given it was about a year after mum's funeral and the first time I had seen my brother since then, that we talked about our mother and our feelings about her death. I think it was probably more a case of my brother wanting to talk, as I was quite happy, having come to terms with it.

Since I was there for a week and we had plenty of time, our conversations moved from mum's funeral to her life, which then transformed into talking about our lives growing up as a family. Once started down that path we then ended up talking about our lives in general. I am the 4th child out of 5 and having very strong personalities in the siblings older than me (the oldest and most dominant was the brother I was talking to at the farm) I ended up being a shy person. As such, I rarely, if ever, spoke to anyone in my family about personal issues. This then expanded into not talking with them about anything I did beyond broad brush stroke details. All of that changed during that week at the farm. I was now old enough, confident enough in myself, and finally in such a sound mental state that I was happy to talk about my life with my brother.

Of course, I also had to point out to him that one reason nobody in the family knew much about my life was that nobody had ever asked. Unlike the others, who were happy to share everything they did with the family, even if we didn't ask or wanted to know, I wouldn't, and to be honest, I don't know that I would have even if they did ask. Anyway, during our conversations each day my brother finally started asking questions. It was during this time of recounting my life and what I had done that I realised, although my depression was real and still there, there was a lot I had done that was truly wonderful, interesting, and worth celebrating, both bad and good. They weren't spectacularly world-changing, but they were mine and they made my life a story worth living.

On the drive home at the end of the week, I started thinking about more of the events I had experienced and the list soon became quite long.

In the following year, I also noticed that I was relating a lot more of my past experiences and stories with my colleagues at work as we went about our day. So much so that at one point I figured I should cut them back a bit, as the others didn't seem to have quite the same volume of stories to tell. It took a while but I realised that was because I was older than they were and as such had clocked up a lot more stories just through sheer age.

Both these situations of recalling moments made me realise that my life has amounted to something worthwhile, certainly much more than my depression was telling me. To keep this self-realised therapy going I decided to write them down, forcing myself to remember what made my life worth living and helping to relive the joy, and sadness, of these moments once again.

I still have depressive episodes but they are nowhere near as extreme as they use to be. I put this improvement down to now appreciating just how good my life has been by remembering events from my past.

# Moments in a Life

After I finished writing the bulk of them down (there are new moments I remember almost daily, so it will never be finished) I decided to put them together into a book. This book. Superficially it is a celebration of my life, but what I am hoping is that by relating my stories I might just inspire others to do the same and help them realise just how good their life has been and continually will be.

I only wish I had done it sooner.

Although it details aspects of who I am and what I have done, it is not an autobiography in the sense of telling the story of my life (there is a LOT I have left out) and the stories are not necessarily in chronological order, but that doesn't matter. What does matter is that these events are all real, to the best of my recollection, and have helped create what in hindsight I think has been an amazing life, just minus the fame.

The stories themselves have been broadly collected into subject areas, rather than a lineal progression through my life. That means I continually jump back and forth, depending on where the particular story fits into the rough subject area.

To give some context to later stories in the book, *Part One: Chronology*, talks about stories from my years growing up, my education, and some of the more interesting jobs I have had.

This then leads into *Part Two: Life*, where I talk about some more general stories. Since I now don't have to keep mentioning where the various places and times fit in, the stories in *Part Two: Life* tend to jump around in order to fit into the broad chapter headings.

And finally, *Part Three: Passion*, delves into my love of all things to do with science, especially astronomy, and sharing this passion with other people.

Hopefully, you will be able to follow my story.

**Rod Somerville**
March 2023

# Part One
# **Chronology**

Moments in a Life

# CHAPTER 1
# Growing Up

---

**Turramurra**

The first memories I can reliably count on involve living in a small, old, wooden house in the affluent Sydney suburb of Turramurra in the early 1960s. My grandparents started renting the house before the Second World War and at the time rents were controlled, especially for returning veterans. This turned out to be a double-edged sword, as their rent essentially never changed, even 40 years later, but it did mean the owner of the property was reluctant to make any improvements or provide more than the minimum maintenance to the house. Any maintenance tended to be done by either my father or my uncle. For instance, when the electrical wiring throughout the house needed replacing it was my uncle, an electrician, that did it, not the landlord.

The house may have been small and a bit rundown, but it did have charm, especially since it is forever associated with the memories of my grandmother. It consisted of a front veranda where my grandmother would sit, watching the world go by, 2 small bedrooms at the front of the house, a kitchen constantly filled with the smell of cooking scones from the gas stove, a small lounge room, a bath/laundry room that was perpetually dimly lit and hot water provided via a gas heater situated over the bath, and a closed-in back veranda area. The toilet was in a spider-filled outhouse halfway up the backyard.

Apart from the outside toilet, the backyard also held an old shed. This was essentially nothing more than a disaster waiting to happen, especially with small children around. Realising this dilapidated death trap had to go, my father and brothers eventually knocked it down and in the process of cleaning it out came across boxes and boxes of old 78 rpm records that must have belonged to my grandparents. Unfortunately, at the time they were deemed not worth keeping. I now wish they still existed as I would love to be able to give them life once again.

The yard itself was big. Much bigger than you would ever find in Sydney these days. The back section housed small garden beds of vegetables and a Choko vine. I know a lot of people aren't fans of the humble Choko, but we used to eat a lot of them, as this vine was quite prolific, and even to this day, I don't mind the occasional baked Choko.

There was also an old Mandarin tree near the toilet. To me, it always seemed to have ripe fruit on it and I picked many a mandarin to eat simply because they were so delicious. For this reason, I think the Mandarin is my favourite fruit.

There was also a large Jacaranda tree, perfect for young children to climb, although, looking back now, I wouldn't recommend anyone over the age of 10 climb a Jacaranda as they don't have the strongest of branches.

In a more surreal image from my memories of the house, down one side there were a number of Privet trees. In the fork of one of them was a toy truck that I am guessing once belonged to one of my older brothers. For some reason, he left it there, and as the years passed, and the tree slowly grew, the truck gradually became more and more consumed by the tree. By the time I noticed it, the truck was no longer able to be removed, and by the time my grandmother died and we left the house for the last time, the truck had almost disappeared. I didn't think about it at the time, but I now wish I had cut that part of the tree out and kept it, or at the very least, taken a photo of it, as it represented to me the passage of my childhood.

The house in Turramurra was where my mother's parents lived but I wasn't very old when my maternal grandfather died, so I don't have many memories of him. To me, the house will always be associated with just my grandmother. I will always remember her sitting on the front porch, enjoying the sun. Or in the kitchen cooking scones. Or picking her up every Sunday to take her to lunch with the family.

One memory, that still shocks me today, is calling in one day and noticing a distinct smell of gas in the house. When I mentioned it, my grandmother told me it was because she had left the gas on overnight in the kitchen. When she woke that morning and realised what had happened, she held her breath and went into the kitchen, turned the gas off, and opened the window to let the gas out. The smell I encountered was the residual of the gas that hadn't yet dissipated. To put this into perspective, at this stage my grandmother struggled to walk without assistance, and certainly couldn't do so very fast. So to get from her bedroom to the kitchen would have taken her a long time and required a considerable effort, all while holding her breath. I didn't do it often, but this particular time I felt I had to chastise her for not getting out of the house and calling for assistance, rather than risking her life by going into a gas-filled kitchen by herself.

As for my father's parents, I never knew my paternal grandmother as she had left long before I was born. My paternal grandfather lived in the inner-city suburb of Willoughby and died when I was still quite young, so again, I don't have many memories of him. I can, however, remember visiting him in his house and every time thinking it smelt like an old man and that it had never been opened up to let in fresh air.

**Berowra**

Like a lot of people, when my parents first married they didn't have much money, so, in order to save on rent, they lived with my mother's parents in their small house. I guess at first it was manageable, but when the family grew to 5 children (I am number 4 on the list), space was becoming an issue. I still have quite vivid memories of us kids sleeping in bunk beds out on the veranda with sheets strung up to act as room partitions.

With the house only big enough for 2 people to live comfortably, but now housing 9 people (2 grandparents, 2 parents, and 5 young children), it was time for our family to move out. I was 4 years old when we finally relocated into our new house in the suburb of Berowra on the northern limits of Sydney.

In the early 1960s, Berowra was very much on the outskirts of the city. It was lightly populated, surrounded by bush, and most of the roads were still unpaved. Facilities were scarce and to do any shopping required travelling to another suburb 8 kilometres away. The particular location of our house was about 2 kilometres off the Pacific Highway and in a newly opened up area. There were perhaps only a handful of houses further along the dirt road than ours.

Of course, initially mum and dad had just bought a block of land, so before we could move, the land had to be cleared and a house had to be built. The block itself was situated near, but not at, the top of a ridge, so the land sloped a little bit. This meant the house was quite a bit higher off the ground at the back than it was at the front. It also meant the backyard sloped. Consequently, in order to make the yard a useful space for young children to play, my father spent an enormous amount of effort constructing retaining walls out of gigantic sandstone blocks. Where he got them from and how he moved them around I still don't know. I was too young to care about those sorts of things at the time, so as a child I never thought to ask. But, as an adult, I am in awe at what he achieved. Once the walls were constructed he then set about backfilling them, eventually making the yard into 2 level areas.

Although it was a builder that constructed the house, it was my father who did a lot of the finishing work. He was the one who painted it, built a railing on the front porch, landscaped the garden, and constructed other finishing touches. I guess in an effort to save some money. Plus, he did this all while still actively working in the centre of the city.

It was during one of these finishing jobs that he had a rather nasty incident. Since the block was essentially in the bush, there was still all manner of creatures hanging around that are readily found in bushland. While constructing a concrete step into the laundry, located under the house, he came across one of them, a scorpion, and was stung. This caused him immense pain and required my mother to rush him to the closest hospital, located 20 minutes away. With 5 young kids, not one of them old enough to drive yet, it meant either putting all of us in the car, which would have taken valuable time, or leaving us in the care of my eldest brother. Rather bravely, I feel, my mother left us in the care of our oldest sibling. You have to remember that this was 30 years before the invention of the mobile phone, so it wasn't so easy to organise a neighbour, even if we had one nearby, to come and watch us. My father had to stay in hospital overnight and take a few days off work, but thankfully he recovered. He was, however, extra careful when turning rocks and other objects over after that.

Our house now had 4 bedrooms, a large living room, dining room, and kitchen. Something that always intrigued me though was that we still only had one bathroom and one toilet, thankfully separate, for 7 people. How we managed to make it work, I don't know, but somehow we did. Of course, there were always the obligatory shouts from just outside the bathroom or toilet door to hurry up and get out, but we survived.

As an aside, our toilet was involved in an intriguing moment in interior design mistakes. When the room needed to be repainted, for some unknown reason my mother left it up to my father to not only paint the toilet walls, but also select the colour. The problem was that my father was colour blind. He chose a colour that he liked, and while we were all out one weekend day, he went to the hardware store, bought the paint, and painted the toilet walls. On returning we discovered that to him it was a pleasant shade of blue that he had picked. To us, however, it was a hideous bright orange. Unfortunately, it stayed that colour until my parents sold the house. Why, I don't know. It wasn't that big a space to repaint, but somehow we never got around to doing it, so for decades, every time we went to the toilet, we had to stare at the worst possible colour you could paint a wall inside a house.

Under the house there was a lot of space. The land sloped enough that at the back edge of the house it was more than high enough to have the laundry, although, being so high meant we had to have 2 flights of stairs in order to get down to the yard. Consequently, the temptation to build another room under the house turned out to be irresistible to my father.

The first stage in the room construction required removing some of the brick pillars holding the house up and replacing them with steel beams. The workmen who did this simply knocked the pillars over, leaving them in big, bricky chunks. My father, never one to waste or throw anything away, decided that the bricks could potentially be used again for something else (who knows what he had in mind) and so it somehow became my job to manually split the individual bricks off the large conglomerations using a hammer and cold chisel. Once a brick was off, I then had to try and clean the remaining cement from it as best I could. I don't think I ever completed the entire job.

The next stage was to dig the floor out and make it level. It may have been high enough at the back of the house, but the ground sloped upward the further you went towards the front. So, having a ready-made workforce of 5 kids, dad quickly put us to work digging out and removing the dirt from under the house. Unfortunately, the dirt was only part of the problem. Not far down we struck a rocky outcrop that required having to get in a specialist. Of course, it was still up to us kids to remove the broken rock, but at least we didn't have to break it up.

Once that was completed, we had to concrete the floor. The day came when the cement truck arrived and it was all hands on deck. Unfortunately, the truck could only get so close, which meant it could only pour the concrete into just one place under the house. In hindsight, the truck driver could have helped us by not dumping the entire load in one steady stream. If I was to do it again now I would certainly tell the driver to stop at regular intervals. However, we didn't back then, and once the concrete started flowing it wasn't stopping until it was all out of the mixer. I can still remember the mad scramble of the entire family frantically shovelling concrete from one spot so it covered the entire area. I don't think I have ever been so tired and sore from one hour's worth of work since.

With the major components now done, it took around 6 months for my father to slowly finish building the room. That required constructing walls, installing plumbing, putting in a glass sliding door, painting the entire room, and various other aspects associated with a large family room. By this stage, my elder brothers had moved out, so it was left to me to be dad's lackey. Eventually, it was finished and over many years it was extensively used for parties, as a games room, and occasionally as an extra bedroom.

Life in a large household needs to be well organised in order to function and ours was no different. Dad would get up every workday morning at 6 am and mum would drive him to the train station to catch the 7 am train into the city. Just before they left she would wake us kids and we would take turns in having a shower, having breakfast, and getting ready for school. Once we were all off to school mum would then start the daily chores.

At the other end of the day, mum would start cooking dinner, timing things so that it would be ready by the time she returned from picking dad up from work on the 7 pm train. While she was gone it was up to us kids to make sure the dinner didn't burn and heaven help us if we didn't watch things like a hawk.

Depending on whether the train was on time or not, mum could be gone for anything between 15 and 20 minutes. During this time my brothers decided to create a fun game for them to play. At least, fun for them, not so much for me.

I am and have always been, extremely ticklish. This has led to being tortured by my siblings many times on an irregular basis. However, one evening, while my mother was picking up my father, my 2 brothers decided to make it into a regular sport. Each night, within minutes of mum leaving, one of them would hold me down in the hallway while the other tickled me. I would try and fight back but they were older, bigger, and stronger than I was, so it was to no avail. After 5 minutes of enduring this agony, they would then carry me down the back stairs and lock me in the laundry for another 5 minutes as I tried in vain to break the door down through sheer anger. They were then smart enough to let me out and stay out of my way, giving me just enough time to calm down, before mum and dad arrived home. This went on for a few years until it suddenly stopped.

For a long time, I didn't understand why until it occurred to me one day that I had gone through a growth spurt and they must have realised I had become big enough to cause them serious harm if they continued with the practice, so they stopped. Many years later, as I told the story at a family gathering, I was shocked to find out that my brothers don't remember the game they played. It was quite a traumatic experience for me so I will never forget it, but apparently, it didn't mean much to them. They have apologised for doing it but I am still amazed that they have no recollection of that part of our shared lives.

Apart from 2 older brothers I also have an older sister. Although she wasn't involved in any games revolving around torturing me, she was involved in one of the more sudden and shocking events of my teen years.

Beside our house was a vacant block of bush set aside because it was a natural watercourse. This was a great place for young kids to explore and play while still having the relative safety of home close by. On the edge of this bush area was a large gum tree and over one of the branches our father had slung a rope to create a swing made out of an old car tyre. For a number of years, the swing provided hours of fun, but on one fateful day, things took a nasty turn.

One of the favourite things to do on the swing was to sit in the tyre and have someone else wind it round and round and then let go. The swing would then start to spin rapidly as it unwound and the person in the tyre would become dizzy before it finally came to a stop. Often, the person being spun would experiment with extending their arms and legs or bringing them in close to moderate the rate of rotation. This was long before I knew about the conservation of angular momentum, but it was fun to play with it and wonder why. Anyway, one day my sister was in the tyre and I was winding her up. She had long hair and unbeknownst to us her hair had become twisted in the rope. Suddenly, the aging rope snapped and my sister fell onto the ground, still sitting in the tyre. Both of us were shocked by the suddenness of the event but otherwise okay, until my sister realised that her hair had been caught in the twisted rope above the breaking point and as she fell it had ripped out a circular patch of her hair about 15 centimetres across. Once that realisation kicked in she started screaming, attracting my mother's attention. And once she saw what had happened I think she became just as panicky and in shock as my sister. It took a neighbour and an hour for both to eventually calm down. Thankfully, her hair eventually grew back.

Decades later my mother and sister commented to me that they had never really thought about how the event might have affected me. They both apologised for that but to be honest, it didn't really affect me all that much. There were far more traumatic events in my life that caused greater distress than something that had occurred to someone else.

One of the great things about living on the outskirts of the city in the 1960s and 70s is that there was never a lack of things to occupy our time. Even if things got really bad we would simply hop on a train and go into the centre of Sydney for no other reason than it was something to do. Of course, back in those days, there was no such thing as helicopter parenting. The instructions when we left home in the morning was simply "be home before dark". Our parents trusted that we wouldn't get into any trouble and that we would be safe. If something did happen then we knew it was up to us to sort it out at the time and get home as quickly as we could.

A classic example of this occurred one day as a group of us were riding our bikes. We used to ride everywhere, including down the busy highway to nearby suburbs and, in this instance, down the steep, narrow and winding road that leads to Berowra Waters, an offshoot of the lower Hawkesbury River. It was about 5 kilometres from the top of the ridge to the bottom and as teenagers, there was no such thing as taking it carefully. It was as fast as you could go all the way down, at least until you got to the hairpin bend near the bottom, and even then it was sometimes easier to simply grab the fence post on the inside bend with one hand and swing yourself around. That way you didn't have to bother braking. Once at the bottom it would then be either swimming in the river or having an ice cream from the local kiosk before starting the long climb back up the hill.

On this particular day, we had been for a swim and had ridden about halfway back. It was hard work and we had to struggle to keep going. Suddenly, the front wheel of my bike came off and I went over the handle bars and landed in the middle of the road, grazed and more than a little confused. Just at that moment, a car coming down the hill came around a blind bend and thankfully managed to stop before running over me as I lay there in the middle of the road. When I got up, with the aid of my friends, I noticed the front forks and wheel on my bike were badly bent. With no chance of fixing it then and there, it meant I had to painfully limp up the remaining 2 kilometres of the hill, carrying my bike. By the time I made it home I was extremely sore, bleeding and weary.

Once I was safe, all I could think of is the wheel must have been loose from the start, so how lucky had I been it didn't come off as we hurtled down the hill and only came off while going slow up the hill. And why up the hill?

A bit of thought on the dynamics of riding a bike explained why up and not down. Going downhill the wheel would have been pushed back into the cradle of the forks while riding uphill required me to put a lot more effort on each turn of the pedals, often causing me to lift slightly on the handlebars, hence allowing the wheel to eventually slip out of its support.

Another incident also involved Berowra Waters.

During one school holiday, I went camping for a few days further up Berowra Creek with 3 friends. To get to the camping spot, we had borrowed a friend's aluminium boat with a small outboard motor (more correctly, we borrowed his father's boat). Our parents had dropped us off at the boat ramp at Berowra Waters and we had organised to have them meet us there in a few days to take us home.

The camping itself went well. The weather was perfect, we had a lot of fun and nobody was seriously injured. But the day we were due to go home a stiff breeze had started. As we steered the boat back along the water and entered a wider section of the creek, we noticed there were quite a few waves stirred up by the wind and the water was becoming increasingly choppy.

There were 4 teenage boys with all their camping gear in the boat, so it wasn't sitting very high in the water and we started to become a bit concerned. We weren't worried about ourselves, as we all knew we could swim the 30 metres to shore if necessary. What we were worried about was all our gear and the fact that we were running out of time to get back to the boat ramp by the allotted time. We decided to press on and, of course, the inevitable happened. The boat started taking on water over the sides from the waves and once that started, everything else happened remarkably quickly. The boat, the outboard motor, our gear, all went to the bottom of Berowra Creek in a matter of seconds. We were all okay and made it to shore without incident, but now we had the problem of what to do. The creek was too deep for us to attempt recovering the boat there and then and our parents by this time were waiting for us at Berowra Waters, so we did the only thing we could do, we started walking.

The bushland was too thick to cut across and make a direct line back to civilisation, so we walked around the shoreline for the remaining few kilometres until we came to the boat ramp. It was an interesting conversation with our parents that day and even now I don't know if my friend's father ever recovered the boat. All I know is my sleeping bag and tent are still somewhere at the bottom of Berowra Creek.

With so much bushland around us, it was natural for my friends and me to explore what we could. Most weekends involved at least one bush trek and virtually everywhere we went there was a creek, cave, or view to explore. Even in the valley just below my house there was a large cave that we frequently visited.

The entire Sydney basin is essentially sandstone, so caves are plentiful everywhere you go that hasn't been developed. A few years ago I visited some caves outside the NSW country town of Narrabri. They were advertised as something worth seeing, but as I walked around them, all I could think about was that the caves within walking distance of my old home in Berowra were far more spectacular. Maybe I had just been spoilt as I was growing up, having a plethora of great caves to explore, but I was unimpressed with the caves outside Narrabri. However, I can recommend visiting them as the views of the Pilliga Forest from the track are well worth the walk.

Another advantage of having Sydney built on sandstone is that there are plenty of Aboriginal carvings scratched into the rocks. A favourite day trip we used to do was to take the track from Berowra train station down to Cowan Creek for a swim. It was a long and winding track through the Ku-ring-gai Chase National Park, but along the way, it passed a flat area of sandstone with several carvings in it. One of them was quite large and pictured an emu. At the time it was just something that was there and it was a convenient place to stop for a break, so we would always have a look at them before moving on. Years later I bought an astronomy poster picturing the Milky Way. Overlaid onto it was an outline of the emu carving I had seen multiple times all those years ago. I still have the poster hanging on my wall.

**Northern NSW**

Eventually, I moved out of home and shared a house with friends. Mum and dad sold the house in Berowra not long after and moved permanently to their property in northern NSW. They had owned the small property, which was a section of my brother's much larger farm subdivided off and sold to them, for some years, but up until then, it was just a holiday home. Situated at the end of a dirt road that has slowly improved from being a rough track when we first started going there, to now being a decent, unsealed road, the farm was the perfect place to visit and relax. It was quiet, beautiful, and had zero light pollution, as the nearest town was about 40 kilometres away. Of a day there was just the sound of birds, wind in the trees, and cattle munching on grass. Wallabies would lazily hop around the yard of an early morning and late afternoon. Once the sun went down the night sky was simply spectacular. There was a spa outside in the yard and one of my favourite things to do would be to sit in the warm spa on a cold winter's night and look at the night sky for an hour or so. Occasionally, when I visited, I would take my telescope to get a closer look at the stars.

Of course, there was more to my visits than just sitting in a spa or stargazing. I would also help out around the property, doing the jobs that my parents were no longer able to do themselves.

Sadly, my father died one day and not long after that mum moved into the nearby town. Looking after the property had become too much for her to do by herself so she moved into a residential house, where she lived for the rest of her life.

## Baulkham Hills

After I moved out of the family home in Berowra, I moved into a shared house with friends I'd met playing Australian Rules Football. It was a large house, which was just as well since there were technically 8 people paying rent who lived there. It may have been a big house, but if everyone happened to be home, then one person had to sleep out in her van. She was the one to sleep outside as she was the last one to join the household and, more importantly, she had a van. We only let her live in the house because she was the sister of one of the others and by the time we had 7 people in the house, what was one more.

One of the great things about living with so many friends was that it was a lot of fun, all the time. One of the downsides was that having so many friends live together it felt like we had to have a party every night, especially if one or 2 other friends visited. It certainly made it hard on our working lives.

I stayed in that house for quite a few years. Different friends would come and go from living there. I moved out for a couple of years in the early nineties to live in Central Australia before moving back in when I returned to Sydney. But eventually, towards the end of the millennium, the owner wanted to sell the house and we all had to move out.

I moved in with another friend, not far from the previous house, and lived there for a few years. But during this time I was becoming increasingly fed up with living in the city. The traffic was terrible, making it difficult and time-consuming to get anywhere, there were too many people, and it was becoming increasingly expensive to live. Things came to a head when one day, on my way to work, I was involved in a traffic incident that turned out to be the final straw.

I lived 23 kilometres from where I worked in the middle of the city. Unfortunately, each morning those 23 kilometres required sitting in bumper to bumper traffic for about 20 of them. A good morning meant the trip only took an hour, a bad morning and it could take almost 2 hours. Trains were not an option as it would require changing twice to get to work and take just as long. Similarly, with buses. Plus, my work hours varied and quite often I wouldn't get home till late at night and sadly, the suburb I lived in wasn't really the safest to be catching public transport to after dark. Plus, another great incentive to drive is that I had free, onsite parking at my workplace.

So, after crawling all the way, the final couple of kilometres required going over the ANZAC Bridge into the city proper. Unfortunately, the 3 lanes of traffic from the west coming over the bridge would then meet with 3 lanes of traffic coming from another direction. We would all meet and blend into just 4 lanes. The ANZAC bridge lanes were on the right, merging with the other lanes on the left. Once merged, the extreme left lane would take you to the northern side of the city, where I worked, the middle 2 lanes into the centre of the city, and the right-hand lane to the south of the city. Since I needed to get to the north of the city but was on the right-hand side of this mess of lanes, it meant I had to firstly merge with one of the lanes from the other direction and then somehow make my way over 2 more lanes to the extreme left.

It was difficult, but generally the slow-moving traffic managed to sort itself out. The first stage was to merge with the other lane. Most people would do the right thing and merge one for one from each lane. However, one particular morning I let the car from my left merge in front of me, and then expected to have the next car in that lane let me merge. Unfortunately, the driver of that van decided he wanted to also squeeze in front of me, even though there was absolutely no room and the car behind me had already dropped back to let him in. With nowhere to go our 2 cars did a slow-motion collision, each scraping the other down the side in an excruciating sound of metal on metal.

I stopped and sat there shocked. He pulled a little in front and then did something bizarre, he got out of his car and, standing in the middle of all this traffic chaos, started to yell and scream at me. He came up to my window and demanded at the top of his voice for me to get out. That was something I was never going to do, as he was obviously in a violent mood.

All this happened in a matter of about one minute and I remember thinking that I was involved in a situation that was literally holding up 10,000 cars from getting into the city. I knew how I felt after having sat in traffic for an hour so I could sympathise with how all these people would be feeling, so close to work but now delayed by a silly act. Since he was obviously unhurt and I knew I wasn't, and both cars at most just had scratches down the side but were still drivable, I figured the best thing I could do was move and let the traffic start flowing again. Miraculously, while he was still yelling at me, a gap opened up, so I took it.

He must have quickly jumped into his van and forced his way into the traffic because within one hundred metres I could see him following right behind me. I figured it was not a good idea to go directly to work, so I drove around the city until he eventually gave up.

A few nights later, I was watching TV at home when a policeman knocked on the door and said I had to call into the city police station, as a report had been made against me. The next day I did just that and was flabbergasted when the officer said that in his report it had been me that got out of the car and yelled at him. Essentially he had changed our roles completely. When I pointed this out to the officer he said that since it was my word against his, nothing would come of the incident, and nothing ever did. Except that I was already fed up with the city and this incident cemented my decision. It was time to get out and leave Sydney for good.

At this point, a friend I first met back in high school rang and suggested I move to a town called Orange, about 250 kilometres west of Sydney. He was currently working there at a local high school as a teacher and there was an opening for an assistant in one of the boarding houses.

## Orange

It was the right move at the right time. Orange is small enough to get around without any problems but big enough to have most things you need. Now that I have lived here for quite a few years I realise that I much prefer living in a country town to living in a large city. The overall standard of living is a lot more relaxed, friendlier, and far less stressful, although, getting used to the colder weather was a challenge I still struggle with. I enjoy occasionally visiting Sydney, but I have to admit that I am always glad to be leaving it after a few days.

For the first 10 years of being in Orange, I lived in a small, one-bedroom flat attached to a school boarding house. However, the time eventually came when I bought a house and moved out.

As it turns out, the friend who suggested I move to Orange had also recently bought a farm, about 30 kilometres out of town. Like me, he was a city boy that had moved to the country, although, he had made the move 15 years before I did. And also like me, he had no real idea of the skills needed to be a successful farmer. However, having recently moved from the city, it was great to get outside and do something physical on the land, although, it took a while to get over the feeling of being dirty for most of the day.

The first thing we had to learn was fencing. How to make a wire fence that could withstand cattle rubbing against it, kangaroos hurling themselves into it, and perhaps most importantly, one that was straight. It may seem like a straightforward thing to construct, but it's not that easy, even after you know what you are doing. Apart from the physical aspect of digging holes for posts, manhandling and cementing in the posts, hammering in countless metal pickets, making sure the pickets are all the same height and in line, and walking back and forth multiple times feeding wire through them without ending up in a complete tangle, there was the mental anguish of having to deal with barbed wire. As useful as it is, barbed wire is the bane of all people that have ever constructed a fence. No matter how careful you are and how much protection you wear, you will get scratched and bloodied simply by picking it up. It seems to have a life of its own and manages to cut you everywhere. Needless to say, I am not of fan of working with barbed wire and am glad I no longer have to use it anymore.

There was obviously more to working on the farm than simply building and repairing fences. Things like water pumps and infrastructure always needed repairing. Fields needed to be sprayed and ploughed and crops needed to be sown. These last few jobs required learning how to drive tractors of various sizes.

One job that seemed to always need doing was slashing some area, either weeds in a paddock or wheat stubble in preparation for burning. The number of times I have run over rocks with the slasher and needed to repair broken blades and bent guards are too many to remember. It seems every time I used the slasher I would have to repair it or spend an hour removing wire I had accidentally run over and wrapped around the motor. Normally I would say it was just the way things are when using a slasher and everyone has these problems, but one time, we had recently planted a few hundred saplings to try and create a windbreak and a few weeks after I accidentally ran over a couple of dozen trees. I suspected after that incident that maybe my slasher issues were more personal than generic.

One of the more spectacular events on a farm is when you burn off a paddock of wheat stubble. In the process of harvesting wheat, the combine harvester cuts the wheat plant above ground level, leaving behind a field of 20 to 30 centimetre long straw sticking up out of the ground. Before you can plough and plant the next crop, this straw needs to be burnt to clear the way. By the time it is ready to be burnt, the straw is very dry and extremely flammable, so for safety, it is necessary to slash and rake around the edge of the paddock to create a fire break. It is also prudent to have a water tank, pump and hose ready and on stand-by.

The first time we did this was in a paddock of around 100 hectares in size. We took all the precautions and started to walk around the edge, lighting the stubble as we went. We were expecting that we would have to get most of the way around to burn it all, with the fire working its way from the edges into the centre. But after lighting about 50 metres of the stubble, the fire took off and raced over the paddock with such speed that before we knew it, the fire had started to die down due to lack of fuel. It took a few hours for everything to get to the point where we could safely leave it, but the initial burst, where essentially all the stubble in a 100 hectare paddock was burnt, took just a few minutes. To say it was spectacular is an understatement and I now know why it is necessary to spend time making a wide enough fire break around the edges and have a water tank ready to be deployed.

Front veranda of my grandmother's house in Turramurra

Front of the house with a young Frangipani tree hiding the bedroom windows

Rear of my grandmother's house showing the outside toilet in the foreground right

The back veranda, repurposed by my grandmother after we had moved out

One year old me beside a very young Jacaranda tree in the back yard

My grandmother sitting on the front veranda, enjoying the sunshine and watching the world go by

The whole family clearing the block at Berowra

My grandmother and brother clearing the bush from the house block

The Berowra house starts taking shape

The almost finished house from the back
Note the laundry on the lower left and the height of the back of the house

The front of the almost completed house

The sandstone retaining walls and leveling of the back yard were all done by my father

The front of the Berowra house 25 years after it was built

Sandstone cave in the Pilliga region of NSW

View from the walk around the sandstone caves of the Pilliga forest

View from the walk around the sandstone caves of the Pilliga forest

The front of my parent's farm house in Northern NSW

The back and side of my parent's farm house in Northern NSW
Usually the spa was located on the concrete slab that now has the chairs and table

The view from my parent's farm house in Northern NSW

Me pretending I know what I'm doing when it comes to building a fence

# CHAPTER 2
# Education

---

**Primary School**

In the 1960s, living in the northern outskirts of Sydney was like being half in the city and half in the countryside. These days it is well within suburbia, but back then it was still lightly populated. So much so that just one primary school catered for everyone. But as the population grew, a second primary school opened and as luck would have it, right across the street from where I lived.

Complete with an abandoned house, the site was an old orchard and the location of endless exploration for myself and other children of the area. Of course, everything changed once the school opened. We lost a great place to play, but it did mean I no longer had to walk 1½ kilometres to get to school. I now only had to cross the road and jump the fence.

When the new school finally opened, for some reason, instead of simply having the relevant students start the day at the new school, we had to first go to the old school. Then, at lunchtime, we were marched as a group to our new place of learning. I can still remember feeling annoyed at having to walk 1½ kilometres to school, then walk 1½ kilometres to my new school, only to end up 30 metres from where I had started.

A few weeks after we had settled into our new school, complete with that new school smell, the entire student population was shuffled into the only classroom big enough to accommodate us all. There we sat, watching the school's one and only, state-of-the-art black and white television, waiting for one of the most significant events in human history, the landing of Apollo 11. There were no classes that day and we sat for hours watching the television, waiting for the moment. No one even wanted to go to the bathroom for fear of missing it. As it turned out, we sat there for a long time. We knew the astronauts had landed before school started at around 6 am, so understandably the teachers thought they would emerge sometime before lunch. However, unknown to anyone at the time, the astronauts were meant to rest for a few hours before getting out.

As you would expect though, when the Apollo 11 crew finally touched down they were far too excited to rest (who wouldn't be!), so Neil Armstrong decided they would exit straight away. But they had underestimated how long it would take to get into their spacesuits and getting ready ended up taking almost as long as their planned rest break. So when Neil finally stepped out it was now lunchtime and we were getting restless from sitting on the hard floor all morning watching nothing happen. Nevertheless, we were all still there when at 12:56 pm AEST on the 21st of July 1969 Neil Armstrong finally set foot on the Moon. Like everyone else in the world, I will never forget that moment.

Even at the age of 8, I realised this was an enormous event, so I kept every newspaper article of the landing I could get my hands on. I filed them away, thinking that someday I would want them, and my young self was right. On the 50th anniversary of the Apollo 11 landing, I still had the articles and they proved to be immensely useful as part of my professional life.

I should mention that as the years passed there were times when I thought about getting rid of them, especially each time I moved house. But every time I would say to myself, not yet. Now they have been laminated and should survive until long after I don't have any more use for them and it will be up to someone else to decide their fate.

For years after the first Moon landing, I read everything about the world around me that I could get my hands on. It was pre-internet days, so the only way to get information was through books, magazines and the occasional television show. Every so often, I was able to talk my father into taking me to the old Sydney Planetarium at the Museum of Applied Arts and Sciences in the centre of the city, complete with a life-sized mock-up of the Apollo Lunar Lander at the front entrance. I loved it, as I'm sure a lot of people did.

I also became an avid fan of science fiction stories and television shows. Over the years, I built up an impressive library of some of the greats in science fiction. Isaac Asimov, Arthur C Clarke, and Ray Bradbury being some of my favourites. Most of them are still sitting in the bookshelves behind me as I write this, although I did get rid of quite a few during one particularly bad depressive episode and I now regret it. I was also a super fan of the television series, *Lost in Space*. I liked *Star Trek*, but for some reason *Lost in Space* was the one I couldn't miss each week. Looking at them today they are quite corny, but for a young boy so soon after the last Apollo mission, they were exciting.

Since this was well before the internet and the enormous amount of information it provides, this obsession with science fiction stories and television shows is what fuelled my hunger for all things science and pointed me towards my future. Looking back, I realise it would have been easy for my parents to squash this fascination as nothing useful, but instead, they supported and nurtured it, and for that, I am eternally grateful. I'm sure my father didn't like *Star Trek* and *Lost in Space*, but he still let me watch them whenever I could and sat there watching them with me.

As a related aside, 20 years later I had a colossal geek moment. While working in Central Australia conducting tours of the night sky, my evening constellation talk involved pointing out the Southern Cross and its 2 Pointer stars. I would mention that the Pointer furthest from the Cross is a star we should all get to know a bit better as it is the closest star system to the Sun, Alpha Centauri. I would then say something along the lines of "Dr Smith has a lot to answer for as they got lost trying to get to the closest star but somehow managed to visit dozens of others along the way". Some people would get the reference. Most didn't. But one night, after making my *Lost in Space* comment, a gentleman came up, thanked me, and then told me he once worked as the set designer for the show. We spent the next half an hour being geeks and talking all things *Lost in Space*.

As the years progressed in Primary School, we were extremely lucky to have a teacher who had obviously done a lot of gymnastics in a previous life. Not only was he a very good classroom teacher, but he was also very good at teaching gymnastics to 12 year old students. He did it all outside of class hours, usually during lunchtime, and I'm sure quite a few people now would be aghast at what he taught us back then. The school had a vaulting horse, a couple of thin mats, some climbing bars cemented into the hard ground, and that was about it. Even so, he taught us how to scale walls 3 times our height, vaults from simple ones just getting over the horse to complex tumbles, and moves on the bars you see in professional gymnastics competitions. All of this done with essentially no safety gear and just him acting as the support/safety person. He had quite a few students and to my knowledge, not a single one of us suffered any injury worse than a sprain and, at times, wounded pride. It was a fantastic thing to learn and although there is no way I could ever do it now I will always be grateful to him for spending the time with us.

Throughout Primary School, another boy and I would alternate between being Dux each year. He eventually went on to be an ambassador for Australia to a major country, and in our final year of Primary School, I was made School Captain. I didn't realise it at the time, but this would be a trend that continued into High School.

## High School

Even as a big fish in a small pond at Primary School I knew High School was going to be a completely different situation and I would be starting as a nobody at the bottom of the schoolyard pecking order. It scared me, as I was going from a co-ed Primary School of 300 students to an all boys school of 1,200 students. Even though I have 2 older brothers, they went to a different school and my sisters went to the all girls school on the other side of the railway line. That meant I would know relatively few people, only my friends and the other boys from my year at Primary School. In a lot of ways, my fear turned out to be justified.

Going to high school in the 1970s was difficult. It didn't help with the transition to the larger school when our year had a delayed start as one of the blocks of classrooms had been burned down over the summer holidays due to arson. It wasn't quite finished being rebuilt by the start of the school year so there weren't enough classrooms to accommodate the entire student body, hence our delayed start. Once the block was finished and the extra classrooms became available, we were able to commence.

When we did eventually start Year 7 (or 1st Form as it was known back then), life wasn't easy. As the youngest, smallest and newest additions to the school, we were considered easy pickings for some of the older boys wanting to display their insecurities through bullying.

One strategy we collectively learnt very quickly was we would assemble in a singular group every recess and lunch, all 200 of us, for protection. Being picked on and drawn into fights was just part of everyday school life back then, but being in a circle meant those in the middle could enjoy a reasonably peaceful break. Each day the outside population would change, so everyone got a chance to enjoy lunchtime at some stage.

These days, something like that would never be tolerated, but back then it was just the way it was. However, some positive outcomes did come from this situation. It created a circle of close friends for me and I decided early on that when we became the older boys at the school we were going to change things and not let the same behaviour occur. Of course, before that could happen there were a number of years to suffer through.

I have always been taller and a larger build than the average for my age group. In Year 7 this made me stick out from the rest and for some reason, this seemed to be an excuse for a boy in Year 10 to single me out for targeted bullying. Every time he walked past he would punch me in the head, be it in the playground, on the bus, on the train, or just walking down the street. It became so bad that I would constantly keep a nervous look out for him wherever I was and avoid drawing his attention in any way possible. For the entire year, I kept thinking that all I had to do was survive that one year, as I knew there was no way he would continue on to Year 11. Thankfully I was correct and I never saw him again. The situation did, however, solidify my resolve to change the culture in the school if at all possible, as well as my resolve to never tolerate bullying again, either towards myself or towards others.

Of course, by the time I reached the age of 15 I was physically larger than most of the older boys, so they were less likely to consider even trying to bully me. As I grew older and became one of the leaders in the school, this apparent immunity also allowed me to enact my earlier resolution of intolerance to bullying among the student body and fundamentally change the school's culture for the better.

I guess it was this determination to change things that also made me stand out as a leader in the school. Starting in Year 11 I was made a prefect and when Year 12 rolled around I was upgraded to being the school captain.

Unfortunately, I am fundamentally a very shy person and being school captain doesn't really allow you to hide in the background. Every time I had to speak in front of the student body or attend official functions I was extremely nervous. If I had to give a speech I would write it and then agonise over it for days, constantly reading and rereading it to make sure it was alright and that I knew it off by heart. Even so, when the time came, I always felt like simply closing my eyes and passing out.

Given my acute shyness, I often thought about why I accepted the position when it was offered and I think it all boils down to a simple case of I am easily, and cheaply, bought.

At the end of Year 11, the incoming school captain is presented with an award of quite a few books, solely for being school captain. The lure of having a generous voucher to select books of my own choosing at the local bookshop was a bribe that momentarily overrode my shyness, so I accepted the position. Plus, at that stage I didn't have to do anything, so the fear of public speaking seemed a long way off in the future.

As school captain there were the usual school-based things I was required to do, talking at assemblies for various events, give speeches at different parent-based functions, and chair meetings, such as the student council. But, perhaps the scariest thing I had to do was at the end of Year 11, not long after accepting the role of school captain. I had to be the Master of Ceremonies at the end of year award day in front of the entire student body and their parents. I was so nervous that the entire few hours were a complete blur and seemed to pass in the blink of an eye. All I can remember from that day is that I had everything I had to say written down word for word in front of me and I must have read it all correctly as no one commented on any mistakes afterwards.

Another aspect of being school captain was I had to represent the school in official external functions. These could be something as simple as media commitments, to representing the school at the gathering of the local high school's captains and vice-captains. These were held every couple of months at a different school in the district and I guess were designed to try and foster friendly relationships between the public and private schools in the area. I don't know how successful they were as I can't remember any of the people I met at those meetings and I can't remember any time where the schools had to interact beyond those meetings and the occasional sporting event. The biggest memory I do have of them was walking into the library (where they were typically held) of one of the private schools and being assaulted with the sight of their brand new, and very bright, lime green carpet. I have never seen so much lime green before or since and I am sure I don't want to. It overwhelmed the senses and all I can remember is thinking to myself, how does anyone get any work done sitting in this library.

One of the more exciting functions I had to attend was having morning tea with the Governor of New South Wales at the time, Sir Roden Cutler, and his wife, Lady Cutler, at government house in Sydney. It wasn't just me, each year the captain and vice-captain from every high school in the Sydney region were invited for morning tea, and as you can imagine, there are a lot of high schools in the area, so there were a lot of people attending.

We had to assemble outside and line up in the order given to us by the organisers and then one by one we were announced and introduced to the Governor and Lady Cutler. How they maintained interest to the very end of the long line of introductions was impressive. What was even more impressive was that once the introductions were over and we all had our cup of tea and cake in hand and mingling in the grounds of Government House, they went around and casually chatted with everyone, including myself, right up to the very end of the function. Admittedly our chat was only for a few minutes, but it was more than a simple hello. They asked about the school and myself before politely taking their leave and moving on to the next person, the whole time appearing to be genuinely interested. I will never forget that function and the example shown by Sir Roden and Lady Cutler on how to be kind, interested, and manage people professionally, regardless of their social standing, even if you are the governor of NSW talking to a schoolboy.

One final thing before leaving my time in high school. As was the case in primary school, I was in the top-level class for all of my subjects for my entire schooling career, and if not dux each year, at least second. But as a sign of how much effort I gave the subject at the time, I was in my one and only B class for English in Year 12. Even now, that annoys me, as it means I didn't give the subject my full attention and maximum effort. At the time it really annoyed me as I saw it as a failure on my part, and when it came time to move on from high school and into university, I vowed never to let that happen again. No matter how difficult the subject was, I would make sure I passed every one. Anything less would be a waste of time and effort and show I had not given it my full devotion.

**University**

Life at university was both scary and exciting. Most of my friends from high school that went to university had decided to go to Sydney University, located in the heart of the city, while only a handful of us had chosen the closer Macquarie University. Of those that went to Macquarie, I was the only one doing a science subject. This meant that I rarely saw the others. There were 2 reasons for this, the first being that they had classes on the other side of the campus, and the second was that they had a lot less face to face hours than I did. My timetable was effectively the same as a full-time working week. Every day my first lecture would start at 9 am and my last would end at either 4 pm or 5 pm. The occasional hour during the day that was free from lectures would usually be spent working on assignments with others from my classes. The only time I would get to see my high school friends was during lunch.

In hindsight, lunches were an interesting time. If there wasn't a band playing in the amphitheatre while you sat on the grassy area in the centre of the university eating your lunch, debates were being held by the law students. These debates usually involved discussions about topics that nobody eating lunch was interested in, so it was more an exercise in public speaking for the law people. Like everyone else, especially the science students, I never gave them much attention, but I can always remember that at the end of the debate they would say "if you agree, move over to the left and if you disagree, move to the right". Of course, nobody was listening and consequently, nobody moved, but this didn't stop them as they would then simply split the grass area down the middle and count how many people happened to be sitting on each side. They would then declare a winner based on these numbers. I may never have listened to the actual debate, but I always thought it was great theatre.

The bands that would sometimes play were unknown at the time and hence trying to make a name for themselves. A lot of them included students from the university who had organised a free gig to get them some exposure. At the time they were a welcome musical addition to a lunch break, providing relief from intense study and I often thought some of them weren't too bad. But since I was focused on my studies and always thinking about the next lecture, or the next assignment, I only ever gave them passing consideration. Looking back on it now, I wish I had paid more attention to those bands giving free concerts as some of them were named Mental As Anything, Midnight Oil and INXS.

University itself was great. I thoroughly enjoyed every minute of my time there. New friends, new experiences and the chance to delve into subjects that had always fascinated me created an environment that I thrived in. My initial reason for choosing the subjects I did was ultimately to become an astrophysicist, so with that in mind I picked every physics subject I could, but, in order to do those, I also had to take some mathematics. Although my passion was physics, I had always loved mathematics, so as I took the requisite maths courses at university I found I enjoyed them just as much as the more physical ones. By the time I reached my final year, the only subjects I did were either maths or physics based and at that point I was working towards getting a double degree in both.

I have to admit that I really enjoyed the combination of playing with high tech equipment like lasers and telescopes in the laboratories and then sitting in lectures thinking about purely intellectual concepts and equations.

The feeling of achievement when I finally completed my undergraduate degrees was immense. So much so that I started my Masters degree in physics, fully intending on progressing onto my Doctorate in Astrophysics. Unfortunately, life has a funny way of diverting the best-laid plans and while studying for my Masters degree my career took an unexpected turn that would define my working life from that moment onwards.

Front page of a newspaper from the time of the Apollo 11 moon landing

A young me posing for an official Primary School photo

Hard at study for a university physics assignment

# CHAPTER 3
# Working Life

---

Like most teenagers, I had the occasional job while at high school. My very first one was at the age of 15 as a storeman in a large clothing store, nothing spectacular, but it did earn me some money. Not a lot, but some. It was also only for the summer break, so it didn't last very long.

**Paper Boy**

The first job that provided a steady income and lasted for about a year occurred while I was in Year 12. At that time, the local, free newspaper was delivered to every household by young kids. My job was to deliver bundles of the newspapers to the houses of these kids in the early hours of Wednesday morning. The kids would then walk around their local neighbourhood that afternoon delivering the individual newspapers.

The day would normally start with a 1 am wakeup in order to be at the pickup site in a neighbouring suburb by 2 am. Each week there would be a list of addresses and how many newspapers to leave at each. The newspapers were bundled into groups of 50 and 25 lots, so it was easy enough to count out the amount required to pick up and be left. I would load as many as I could into my car, often pushing the suspension to its limit, and each week I wished that I had a ute, instead of my sister's old hand me down car. It would have made things so much easier if I had been able to fit all of the newspapers into one trip, but, having the small car that I did, it often meant making at least 2, if not 3, trips back to the main pile for collection.

Starting at 2 am and finishing the deliveries around 6 am meant that Wednesdays were long. I would have just enough time to get home, shower, dress, and eat breakfast before heading off to school for the day.

They made for long days but there was also something really enjoyable and peaceful about driving around the area without any of the usual activity and without any rush to get things done as quickly as possible.

**Garbage Collector**

Once I started university my parents began subtly hinting I needed to start paying for myself more than I was. I even think at one stage the dreaded word 'rent' was mentioned. Consequently, in my first year of university, I got a job during each holiday period that I don't think you will find in any careers pamphlet.

A friend of my parents had the contract to pick up the garbage from the various beaches, islands and leisure boats located around the shore of Pittwater, Broken Bay and the lower reaches of the Hawkesbury River. This involved driving a small, flat bottomed barge around to all the little beaches, collecting the garbage in wool bale bags and bringing them back to the truck located at Brooklyn, a small town on the banks of the Hawkesbury River. We would then take the truck to the tip to empty, ready to do it all again the following morning. During school holidays, especially the summer break, there were a lot more people on the water and hence a lot more garbage to collect. Normally my parent's friend could do it himself, but during these busier times, he needed help, hence employing me, as my university breaks coincided nicely with the times he needed assistance.

Before I could start I needed to get my boat license. After a day of reading up on the rules and a quick test the following day, I had my license, still no real practical experience in driving a boat, but I at least knew the rules.

The day would start at 6 am and usually be over by 1 pm. During winter, these hours were not very pleasant, but during summer, it was a spectacular time to be on the water. Warm, sunny, and thoroughly enjoying pottering around the bay in a small boat, I couldn't think of a better way to spend my summer break.

Since there were a lot of boats filled with holidaymakers utilising the isolated beaches and inlets found around the bay, we would often collect the garbage directly from a boat. As well as handing over their rubbish, they would usually also give us a few bottles of beer. By the end of the day, we had quite a stash to take home, although some didn't quite make it that far.

The setting was magnificent. The job itself, not so much. As I mentioned earlier, the job entailed taking a small, flat bottomed barge with twin outboard motors around to all the little beaches, bays and boats, collecting any garbage. There are a lot of little beaches with large garbage bins around Pittwater and Broken Bay, so it wasn't possible to get to all of them in one day. In fact, it took about a week to complete the rotation and start again. That meant when we did get to a bin it was usually pretty full and been there for at least a few days in the hot, summer sun. We would pull up to a beach, empty the contents of the bin into a wool bale bag, put the bag into the barge and move on to the next beach.

The barge wasn't very big, so after a number of beaches, it was full. So, to minimise the number of times we had to return to the truck to empty the barge each day, we would try and cram as much as possible into the boat. This meant the barge often only had 10 centimetres freeboard (the height from the waterline to the side of the boat) and it meant that at times we had to sit on the bags full of garbage to steer the boat.

The first time I sat on the bags I got a shock when I realised the bag underneath me was squirming. My first thought was a snake but it soon became clear that the squirming was caused by something a little less dangerous, but a good deal more disgusting. Because the garbage, containing a lot of food scraps, had been sitting in the bin for a few days in the sun, it had become more maggots than garbage. When we tipped it into the bag they came with the rest and it was the thousands of maggots that I could feel squirming around under my bottom as I drove the boat. It was a bit hard to deal with for the first week, but after that, it was just something to live with and I soon forgot about it altogether.

With such a low freeboard it put you very close to the water, allowing you to often see the life that teemed under the surface. One of the most spectacular sights was, as I pulled into a little bay to get to the beach, occasionally it would be filled with tens of thousands of large brown jellyfish (*Phyllorhiza punctate*). They were so thick it almost seemed like you could walk across them to get to the shore. This event happened several times when I was working.

Another, more problematic issue with having the side of the barge sit so low in the water is that we weren't able to work if the water was too rough. Thankfully there were only a handful of those days, although there was one time when things started calmly enough but turned into what can only be described as an adrenalin-fuelled trip home.

On this particular day, the weather started calm and sunny. While my boss went to another area of Broken Bay I was sent over by myself to Pittwater. This particular garbage run took the longest, as it involved a long boat ride and had multiple beaches to call into. The trip over was uneventful and I enjoyed the serenity of being alone on the water. However, while doing my collection in the relatively sheltered Pittwater, I didn't notice that a south-easterly breeze had come up.

Any other direction and Broken Bay tends to break up the wind and only cause small, choppy waves, but a south-easterly direction is just right to generate a large swell over the open waters of the bay. As I finally started towards Brooklyn and the end of my day, I realised that Pittwater had become choppy. This wasn't a big problem, but I did think it would make for a tense trip home. Unfortunately, when I got to the end of Pittwater and was able to see the open waters of Broken Bay I could see that the wind had generated a swell roughly 2 metres from trough to peak. This was definitely a huge problem.

I circled around for a while, thinking, weighing up my options, and calculating risks. I couldn't stop anywhere in Pittwater and wait it out, but to travel across the bay was a huge risk, as I only had a few centimetres of freeboard. The waves weren't far enough apart for me to get between a couple and sit there as I made my way across, I would have to travel over them. That prospect then raised the memory of our ill-fated camping trip a few years back when we sunk our friend's boat and had to swim to shore. However, the difference here was that Broken Bay is much deeper than

Berowra Creek, and wider, and full of sharks.

Eventually, I had to make a decision, and with the bravado of youth, I decided I had to try. I was a strong swimmer so figured I could always make it to shore, even if I went down in the middle of the bay. As for sharks, well, I tried not to think about them. Worry about that problem if/when the situation arose.

Getting out into the bay was the first issue. It involved having to cut sideways across the swell until I could straighten up. Nevertheless, I managed to navigate that problem without too many heart-stopping moments.

Next came the long diagonal trip across the bay to get to Brooklyn. If I simply went up and down the waves in the direction they were headed, all I would achieve is moving down the bay without addressing the problem of getting across. Plus, I didn't have enough fuel to go far enough down until the waves reduced in size and then come back up the other side. The only solution I could see was to surf the waves down the leading edge and then power up and over the back of the wave in front of me and surf down it, repeating the process until I made it across the 10 kilometres of open water and into the sheltered safety of Brooklyn.

I don't remember how long it took, but eventually, I made it. I do remember being terrified the whole way but having to remain calm and focused on the job at hand. I think it was the intense concentration required that helped me manage the trip and not panic. Needless to say, I was always aware of weather reports after that day.

**Taxi Driver**

The garbage job was great, but it didn't pay a lot and was only holiday work. What I needed was a part-time job all year round. So, from my second year of university until I finished, I became a taxi driver.

I was at my best friend's house one day, talking to him and his father about having to find a job. His father then floated an idea past both of us that immediately seemed intriguing. He had recently started driving a taxi every Sunday to earn a bit more money and suggested that if we wanted to, he could organise to get the taxi from Friday night for the entire weekend and share it with us. The prospect of doing something that, once again, was different to the usual, run of the mill part-time job immediately interested us. So, after multiple weeks of evening courses in the city learning how to be a taxi driver, we were ready to do our driving tests.

The test itself was nerve-racking. It required driving around the city for half an hour, visiting all the worst traffic spots to see how you handled them, all the while doing everything perfectly. Make one mistake, you failed. Yet, despite the nerves, somehow I managed to fluke passing the test on the first attempt.

Since this was before GPS, mobile phones and all the other technology we now take for granted to help us find our way about, to be a taxi driver meant you had to memorise all the streets in the city, all the main roads in the suburbs and where all the hospitals were. In particular, you had to know the closest hospital and the quickest route to it from wherever you were. If needed, there was always the street directory available, safely tucked away under the seat, but memory was always meant to be your first option.

The 2 shifts my friend and I would do was from 7 pm Friday evening through to 10 am Saturday morning, and 10 am through to midnight Saturday night. My friend's father would then take it for his Sunday shift. The downside of this arrangement was we never got to socialise with each other on a weekend, as we would alternate between the Friday night and Saturday shifts. The upside was we were making some pretty good money.

The shifts were long, but it didn't take much to adjust, as the lure of money made it easy to keep going. There were times when I would be at university all day Friday, drive the taxi all Friday night, stay up all day Saturday and then go out Saturday night until the early hours of Sunday morning. Don't ask me how I could stay awake for the better part of 48 hours, but, as someone only just into their twenties at the time, all I can put it down to is youth. There was, however, one time that weariness got the better of me while driving the taxi.

It was 6 am one Saturday morning. Having just crossed the Sydney Harbour Bridge to drop a passenger off in The Rocks area on the harbour foreshore, I turned into George Street, the central street of the city. After having driven all night I was tired and thought since I was there, I'd make one last trip through the city for a fare before starting to work my way towards home.

At 6 am there's not a lot of traffic in the city and even fewer people.

The only other car I could see was another taxi, about 20 metres in front of me, and the only person in view was a lady who put her arm out to flag one of us down. As the other taxi was in front, I assumed he would pull over to get the fare and I would continue on, looking for another. That was the point my tiredness caused me to come unstuck. I assumed correctly that he would get the fare, but my assumption that he would pull over to the curbside lane (George Street had 2 lanes in each direction) and stop turned out to be incorrect. Although no cars were preventing him from doing so, rather than pull over to the side he just stopped where he was, on the inside lane. Being tired then caused my reaction time to be too slow and I collided into the back of him.

Thankfully, neither of us were travelling very fast so neither of us were injured, but the cars were a little worse for the incident. By the time we had both pulled over to the side and got out of the car, I noticed another taxi had picked up the lady that had been the catalyst for the event.

As we stood beside the cars, the other driver was understandably angry. But the thing I couldn't understand was that he wasn't yelling at me about smashing the back of his car, all he could yell about was that I had made him lose the fare.

At this point, a council street sweeper truck, the type that sprays water to wash everything into the gutter, came along. As we were still standing beside the cars on the roadside and not on the footpath, the truck stopped, turned off the water, and motioned for us to move. I started to move but before I could get far the other taxi driver made a rude comment to the driver who then shrugged his shoulders, turned the water back on and drove past us. So, not only was I being yelled at by an angry man but I was now also soaked with water up to my waist. Eventually, we exchanged details and drove off, however, I figured the incident was enough for me so I drove home and explained to my friend why he couldn't drive his shift that weekend.

There were, of course, plenty of non-accident moments as well. Meeting a wide range of people kept things interesting, especially when a lot of your passengers were picked up in the red light district of the city, Kings Cross. After a certain time on a Friday evening, fares around the outlying suburbs started to thin out. So the natural thing to do is head into the city, especially Kings Cross, as you knew there would always be people around. The problem was that at that time the people you picked up also tended to have been out drinking for quite a few hours. Even so, people were generally well behaved. Those that were well and truly intoxicated tended to have friends that would pour them into the car and give me the address to take them to. Only once did I have someone get in at Kings Cross and ask to go to the nearest hospital because he had been stabbed in the arm during a fight.

In a weird situation, I even got to know some of the prostitutes. I tended to be in the area at the same time each weekend I had that shift and they tended to finish at the same time each week. Consequently, I was often the taxi that picked up the same girls. I didn't mind, as they tended to be the friendliest, most well-behaved passengers I could hope to have at that time and in that location.

## Cleaner

During university breaks, I also did some casual jobs. The worst was the 2 weeks I spent working for a company that hired out worksite offices.

They had a yard full of portable offices that you find on worksites. If somewhere needed an office they would modify the office, which was essentially just an insulated shipping container, to the requirements requested, load it onto a truck and deliver it. Once they had finished with it, the office would then come back into the yard, waiting for the next time it had to go out. And that's where I came in.

My job was to clean the office, inside and out. Given that it had been on a worksite, it was always covered in mud and often splattered with concrete. Dirt is easy to wash off, although it did mean getting extremely wet and covered in mud and detergent every day. Concrete, however, has to be scraped off, and that's not easy. I am so glad the job was only for a limited period, otherwise, I would have had to quit after 2 weeks.

## Physics Tutor

Once I finished my undergraduate degrees, but before I decided to continue with my Masters degree, I needed to work for a year or two.

Since I had just finished being in physics labs as a student, I figured why not continue working in the labs, but this time as a tutor.

As I've mentioned before, I am fundamentally a shy person and that can sometimes manifest itself as feeling like a bit of an imposter and not having confidence in myself and my abilities. Despite this, I applied for a job as a tutor in the first year physics labs at Sydney University and got the job.

The first thing that struck me was that all through my time at Macquarie University the labs only ever had a maximum of 15 students in them, even the first year labs. At Sydney University I was one of 3 tutors wandering around a massive lab that held over 100 students. Secondly, it made me realise how lucky I had been by going to Macquarie and not Sydney University. I am also glad I had that job for the year, as it showed me that I should, and can, have confidence in my abilities. Having to explain things to students made me realise I did know what I was talking about. Although my shyness is a constant battle, that first job in my area of expertise showed me I can do it and gave me the confidence to overcome the shyness in later positions.

Later, while studying for my Masters degree, I got to do it all again, this time in the first year physics labs at Macquarie University and the experience was so much better. Fewer students per tutor in a lot friendlier environment means it is easier to keep an eye on what the students are doing and help individuals when needed.

**Laboratory Assistant**

I can't remember how I heard about the position opening, but the job was for a limited period of 6 months as a laboratory assistant back at my old high school. The job assists the science teachers by preparing equipment for lessons each day and maintaining the labs in a safe state. This was back in the 1980s and the experiments the teachers could perform were a lot more exciting than they are allowed to do today. Controlled explosions, radioactive samples, and blobs of mercury rolling around on the benchtop were all part of a science teacher's repertoire. Chemical reactions using acids were a big part as well.

The acids came in bottles of 10 molar concentrations, far stronger than would ever be used. Typical concentrations required for experiments were 1 molar or less, so that meant the acid had to be diluted. Since the original bottles of acid were such high concentrations they were all safely locked away in a chemical storeroom. The problem was that the storeroom used by the school looked like it had originally been a broom closet. It wasn't very big, and there was little room to move about, barely enough to walk in and turn around on the spot. Due to the cramped space, the larger bottles and the stronger acids tended to be stored on the lower shelves.

One day, I had to get some acid to dilute for a class being held that morning. I went into the storeroom and found the bottle I was after on a lower shelf. However, due to the narrow space, as I bent down to get the bottle, I accidentally knocked a bottle of 10 molar sulphuric acid off a higher shelf, right beside my leg.

I never really believed the stories that in moments of crisis time seems to slow down, at least not until that moment. It isn't that time slows down but more a case that your thought processes speed up dramatically. I can still clearly remember thinking, as the glass bottle fell the one metre from the shelf to the floor: what sort of acid it was, its concentration, the damage that would do to my foot and leg, that I needed to flush the area with water to mitigate the effects of the acid, where the nearest tap was, and how long would it take me to get there. All of this in the space of half a second, before the bottle hit the floor and smashed.

As I watched the bottle hit the ground something happened that I didn't expect, it landed on the edge of its base and didn't break, it bounced. Not very high, but I knew I couldn't let it hit the floor again, so I caught it on the bounce. How, I don't know. I carefully put it back on the shelf and left the storeroom, went back to the main preparation area and sat down, as I was feeling quite faint. The other lab assistant was there and immediately commented on how pale I looked. Apparently, I looked as faint and in shock as much as I felt. The incident didn't stop me from doing my job and going into the storeroom again, but from that day onwards I was extra careful each time I did.

### NSW National Parks and Wildlife Service

Another job was with the New South Wales National Parks and Wildlife Service (NPWS) at Ku-ring-gai Chase National Park on the northern edge of Sydney. Although my background is in physics and mathematics, I love discovering anything I can about the world around me. So, even though the job was very much biological in nature, I enjoyed every moment I was there. Essentially the position was being an assistant to whoever needed help on the day. Most of the work involved being outside, in the bush, so I felt right at home. It reminded me of my younger days exploring the same bushland from my house.

The period I was there happened to be just as the government was planning to build the F1 freeway from Hornsby to Berowra and building it required reclaiming land from the national park. Even though there wasn't anything they could do to stop it, the park management was not only concerned about losing so much of the park to the freeway itself but also the effect the earthworks would have on parts not officially reclaimed.

To mitigate any consequences, they needed to know what was going to be affected and then keep track of them as work was being done. The majority of my work at the park involved helping the rangers with this program.

The first thing we did was a stream survey of all the streams and creeks along the path of the freeway. We located and measured all aspects of the streams we could find. This meant beating our way through the bush, hoping to eventually stumble onto a stream. Once discovered we had to measure its width, cross-section, and flow rate so we could keep track over time on how the waterway was affected and whether it was silting up due to the earthworks of the freeway. Of course these days the job would have been so much easier, as the streams could have been located with satellite imagery and drones. But back then we had to do it the hard way and make our way through the dense bushland on foot.

Another related project was the park needed to know all the vegetation types contained within its boundaries. Initially, it was to keep track of the freeway work and if any species might be lost, but management decided to extend it and create a vegetation survey for the entire park. The people hired to do the work was the National Herbarium, located in Sydney, and, of course, they needed someone from the park to assist them.

The process involved looking at aerial photographs of the park and noting general areas where the vegetation appeared to be different. Once identified, we would drive as close as we could to the designated area and then walk to where we needed to be. Once there, we would string out a 10 metre by 10 metre square and collect samples of every different plant we could find in that 100 square metres. If it could be identified on the spot, we would make a note, otherwise, it was taken back to the office for identification.

In principle, this whole procedure was simple: identify a place, go there, collect samples, return to the office and make a list of plants discovered. In practice, however, it was anything but simple. The bush in Ku-ring-gai Chase National Park is thick, tough, and very unforgiving to try and get through. The whole Sydney region is also made of sandstone and consequently has many cliffs and rocky outcrops. Therefore, making your way through the bush also meant often having to climb up or down cliffs to get to where you wanted to go. Sometimes, the square you wanted to peg out encompassed rocky outcrops and that complicated things no end. It was hot, exhausting work and usually involved being scratched all over, despite wearing protective clothing. Often, we would only get to do one patch in the entire day because of the difficulty in getting to it. Nevertheless, I loved every minute.

One final job I did for the NPWS involved their bushfire fighting reporting form. Their old system was purely paper-based and needed updating. Given my background, I was employed to visit several national parks throughout the state and talk with their fire marshals about changes they thought needed to be made to the form. After collecting all their thoughts and suggestions, I then collated them and produced a new version of the paper form.

That, however, was only the first stage. Once I knew what needed to be included, I then had to create an online version that the fire marshals had access to and could fill out, quickly allowing coordinators in Sydney to see the state of all fires around NSW.

As this was still at the beginning of the computer revolution, there were no pre-existing, form creation programs, so the online version had to be manually coded, a process that took quite a while, and a lot of swearing and cursing until it was finally ready to be deployed.

## Sydney Observatory

While studying for my undergraduate degree, I started to do some public education of science, in particular, astronomy and found I liked it. I wanted to do more. But before I could get too carried away, I had to finish my undergraduate degrees and start my Masters in Astrophysics.

As any university student knows, there is only so long before I was expected to start contributing to my own financial support. My parents were very good and never said it out loud, but I knew I had to start earning more than a few dollars to help support myself. As a means to rectify this situation, my Masters supervisor at university suggested a position he had recently heard about, working in the evening as a science educator on a casual basis at Sydney Observatory. I did not know it at the time, but this was the start of my future career path.

The Observatory had only recently closed as a working facility, and even though it occupies one of the best locations in the city, rather than demolish such a historic and magnificent building, it was transferred to the Museum of Applied Arts and Sciences. That meant it was now a museum and science centre. It was also why they advertised for casual science educators and the reason I now had a job.

As I have already mentioned, I am fundamentally a shy person and find it challenging to engage with strangers, which may seem an odd thing to say as I now had a job talking to continually changing groups of people. But astronomy, and science in general, was my passion and talking about it came easily, so my inherent shyness was not a problem.

The first couple of years working there, I think, finally determined my life. The people I worked with were great, as was the general atmosphere of the place, and converting a working museum full of beautiful old astronomical equipment into a functioning science museum was exciting. I realised that being a science communicator was what I wanted to be, so I left university and went full time explaining science to the public.

Perhaps the thing that really sold me on the change were the friends I made at the observatory. I wasn't the only casual guide initially hired and over time we all worked with each other and all became very good friends. We still are.

Quite often after finishing work around 11 pm, we would go down to Pancakes On The Rocks, an all-night pancake place just down the hill, and talk for a few hours over dinner.

Every New Years Eve the observatory would be closed to the public so all the guides would have a party and watch the fireworks from the top of the observatory's tower. This lasted until the museum's management realised they could make money from doing the same thing with paying customers and banned us from doing it again.

One friend had a crush on Whitney Houston and would play a video of her singing the same 4 songs every time he worked. As we set up for the evening, Whitney would be blaring through the loudspeakers, only being turned off just before opening the doors for the public. It was the same person that on one weekend morning had to build scaffolding across a flooded basement to get to the power box to turn off the power to the entire building. Torrential rain overnight had flooded the basement and a few other places, submerging power points and making the whole building an electrical hazard.

On a sadder note, one guide that had been there since before it converted to a museum, and was loved by everyone, went missing one day. He apparently went swimming in a river on the southern outskirts of the city and was never seen again. His clothes were located beside the river bank but he was never found. Eventually, we had to face the fact that he was gone forever and so all his friends at the observatory had a tree-planting ceremony to remember him. The tree and plaque are still there, commemorating a lost friend.

Since it was still a transitional phase for the observatory, in the beginning, it took a while to get used to showing visitors around what was primarily a working observatory, minus the working part. The building had the feeling that everyone had just stood up and walked out one day, leaving everything behind and giving the building an eerie feel to it, especially at night. When the museum installed some yellow spotlights to illuminate the outside of the building, it didn't help to alleviate this impression. Instead, it just gave the whole site a sickly, slightly horror movie-ish appearance. Arriving at night, I would half expect to see a ghostly figure looking out of the top floor window.

I wasn't the only one who had this impression of the building. As part of the evening tour, each guide would take their group of visitors down to the basement, where we had some instruments and atomic clocks stored. One of the other guides was so spooked by the ambience within the building that whenever it came time for her to go down to the basement, she wouldn't do it. We had to swap groups at that point, and I would end up going downstairs twice each night we worked together. That such a rational, intelligent person would have such a fear always amused us, but we still adored her. To us, it was just one of her quirks.

In the following years at Sydney Observatory, there were the usual school tours, evening tours and adult education courses, but the observatory had now been a science centre for several years and things were expanding. As someone who had been there from the start and possessed a wealth of experience and knowledge, I was closely involved in developing programs and events. It was also one of my tasks to deal with the media.

Over the years, I have been interviewed by TV, radio and print media about all manner of things astronomical. Anything from my thoughts on UFO sightings, to upcoming events held at the Observatory, to explanations of astronomical phenomenon. I have to admit I didn't enjoy the TV interviews, as they tend to edit more severely than other media. Quite often, I came across as not making a lot of sense. Of course, it wasn't just me, they did it to everyone. I did, however, enjoy the radio and print interviews, as I could have a conversation with the reporter and lead the discussion in the direction I wanted it to go.

Occasionally there were more extended, fun interviews with the media. I have appeared in print in an Australian Geographic article, been interviewed for a domestic in-flight magazine, conducted a recorded conversation for in-flight QANTAS radio and, perhaps my favourite, did a weekly series about the planets on ABC Radio. Each week I would talk for 5 minutes on the mythology, facts and figures for a different planet. It was a pity there were only the Sun, Moon and 9 planets (Pluto was still a planet back then) to talk about.

In the beginning, the observatory had just one evening tour, held on a Wednesday, but by the mid-nineties, we had built the observatory up to the point where we were running 2 tours every night of the week, all year round. We had also started school holiday programs, which were specifically for children during the day, but inclusive of adults in the evening. We also started holding special viewing events of an evening. It would be an understatement to say we became creative with our marketing since we were fundamentally doing the same thing each time. However, the programs did manage to create interest and entice people to come and visit the observatory.

Our daytime school programs started at just a couple per week but were eventually built up to 2 every weekday morning during school terms. Public opening hours were initially 2 pm to 5 pm during the week and 10 am to 5 pm on weekends. However, before too long, we had extended them to 10 am to 5 pm every day of the week. We ran regular tours of the telescopes, talking about the instruments themselves and then using them to look at planets and stars during the daytime.

If it happened to be cloudy, our go-to option was an object not quite as celestial, the city. The Sydney Harbour Bridge to the north, traffic on a bridge to the west, a lighthouse to the east, or a city building to the south were favourites. They were far enough away to demonstrate what the telescopes were capable of, but close enough to compare with the view we could see with our eyes.

Like any major city, the traffic in Sydney is appalling and evening peak hour lasts until well after sunset. I lived out west, near Parramatta, and the last thing I wanted to do was sit in traffic trying to get home. So, before leaving, I would use the telescope to check the traffic on the bridge heading west. If it was light, I would go. If it was heavy, I would wait an hour. Either way, I got home at about the same time, so I figured it was better to sit at work than in traffic. It may not have been what the telescope was designed for, but I look at it as an inventive use of a handy tool.

One of the most satisfying aspects of working in a science centre is getting to meet and interact with people of all ages. Most were friendly and keen to listen and learn. But for me, the children who dragged their parents along because they were super keen and wanted to know everything they could about space are what made it all worthwhile, as it reminded me so much of when I was young. In the age before the internet, visiting museums and science centres was often the only way kids could discover things. I have many great memories of talking with children and parents about space, trying to answer their questions.

A child's enthusiasm and appreciation were more than enough to make my day worthwhile, but it was when they sent a letter expressing their gratitude that I would realise how much of a positive impact I could have. Encouraging their eagerness for an hour could make an impression that lasted a lifetime, and all it cost me was a bit of time. Over the years, I have thankfully received a number of these letters, and I still have them to this day.

It was a busy and productive time with special events sprinkled in amongst the daily routine. The observatory had made a conscious decision not to do a lot of outreach programs, despite constant requests, as we wanted people to visit the museum instead. We had a few portable telescopes, so it could have been possible, but we had decided it was better to have people come to us and use the larger telescopes in the domes or the smaller ones in the grounds. We did, however, do the occasional outreach for exceptional events and publicity purposes. Two exceptional events stand out in my memory.

The first was held at the amusement park on Sydney Harbour's northern foreshore, just under the Harbour Bridge. Luna Park had been there since long before I was born, and I had spent many days there in my youth. It was a fantastic place in a fantastic location. Before upgrades were made (I think wrecking the experience) the rollercoaster used to go out over the water of Sydney Harbour. Talk about a great ride. Anyway, one particular night in August 1995, Luna Park organised a special event and called it 'Festival of the Luna'. The observatory provided a telescope and some people, including myself, to operate it with the instruction of placing a particular emphasis on viewing the Moon. The festival only went for one night, but the weather was perfect, and up and until then, I don't think I had ever spoken to so many people in such a short period of time. We had a great night, made even better by receiving free passes to use at the park as thanks for being there.

The second event was at the Sydney Opera House in June 1996, where they were hosting a play about the life of Galileo. I guess as a gimmick they wanted telescopes on the Opera House forecourt for patrons to look through before, after, and at intermission in the play. I suspect it was more good luck than good judgement, but Jupiter was high in the sky at the time, so it was a perfect opportunity to view the planet and talk about how Galileo was the first to see Jupiter's largest moons. We were there over 5 nights (thankfully with clear weather the whole time) with 2 telescopes each night, and as thanks, everyone who worked was given tickets to see the play on the final night. It was a great play in a great location and we all thoroughly enjoyed the week-long experience. After all, who wouldn't enjoy showing people through a telescope on the Sydney Opera House forecourt jutting into Sydney Harbour.

On the first night, there was a moment that still makes me chuckle when I think about it. The Opera House had invited several VIPs, including a world-famous astronomer. We had already shown a few people through the telescope before the play started, so we knew precisely where Jupiter was. During intermission, the astronomer and his friends came out to have a look and as they were looking through the telescope and listening to our explanation, one member of the group asked where Jupiter was in the sky. I pointed at the brightest object visible and said there it is. Even though I had been pointing the telescope at it for a few hours, the astronomer contradicted me! He told his friend I was wrong and that it wasn't Jupiter at all. I was sure which point of light was Jupiter, so feeling baffled and flustered, I started to say please have a look at where the telescope was pointing, but he stuck to his story, insisting I didn't know what I was talking about. When intermission was over, they went back inside, leaving us momentarily alone, and we had a good laugh about it.

This wasn't the only time I have met professional astronomers that don't know their way around the night sky. It seems if you want to know details about an object, ask a professional astronomer, but if you want to locate something, ask an amateur astronomer. Of course, like all rules, there are exceptions.

Without a doubt, however, the best publicity outreaches we did were at Circular Quay on the edge of Sydney Harbour. For 4 hours each sunny Saturday and Sunday over summer, we set up a telescope on the grassy area on the western side of the Quay and used a solar filter to look safely at the Sun. The observatory is at the top of the hill above The Rocks area, while Circular Quay is on the harbour's edge beside The Rocks. By setting up at the Quay, we could do our PR exercise and suggest people walk up the hill and visit the Observatory. I can think of very few better ways to spend a workday than being in the sunshine beside Sydney Harbour watching ferries come and go while talking to people as they peered through a telescope at the Sun.

Getting people to look through a telescope directly at the Sun requires a certain amount of trust. A lot of people weren't merely going to take our word that it was safe, so we soon learnt we had to show it was safe by looking through it ourselves. It was during one of these demonstration times that I had perhaps my best experience using a telescope. At that time the Sun was near the peak of its activity, so there were lots of prominences and flares visible on its surface.

As I was looking through the telescope, I saw a truly spectacular flare occur on the edge of the solar disc. It grew to be about half the diameter of the Sun in size, making it around 500,000 kilometres high. That is impressive, but even more so is that it went from start to finish in the space of just 10 minutes, visibly changing shape and size as I watched in wonder. This was the first, and so far only, large prominence I have seen change shape so dramatically in front of my eyes. I was awestruck. I knew if I looked away, I wouldn't get another chance to see an event like this again, perhaps ever.

Being part of a large museum also gives you the opportunity to participate in other facets the museum has to offer. The Powerhouse Museum, of which Sydney Observatory was a part, had a train they sent all over the state, rarely coming back to Sydney. It had 2 carriages outfitted with an exhibition, one carriage with sleeping and kitchen facilities and a fourth carriage at the rear for storage and a bathroom. The train gave people in rural towns the chance to experience a museum like The Powerhouse without having to go to Sydney.

It was a great success, and it was a shame when the museum closed it down. But while it was still operational, I put my name down for the occasional tour. After a couple of weeks of working on it every day, I would then come home, have 4 days off before going back to my regular job at the observatory. I loved being back under the wide-open skies of rural Australia, but the most vivid memory I have of those trips was of a time when the usually smooth operation of the train had a glitch.

Because the train would go to one town, sit there for a few days and then move on to the next town it wasn't cost-effective for the museum to have a locomotive attached all the time. So the carriages sat by themselves and when it was time to move an engine would come, hook up and transport the show to the next railway station or siding. This usually worked well. We knew when the locomotive would be coming and when it would get to the next town. For safety reasons, staff were not allowed to ride the train when it moved, so that meant we also had a car, allowing us to get around a town and drive to the next destination. We usually packed things up the night before moving, to protect them from being damaged during the trip, but since it only took half an hour to store everything away and this particular time the locomotive wasn't due until 10 am, we figured we had plenty of time to pack in the morning.

But at 6 am we were awakened suddenly by a massive jolt caused by the locomotive attaching itself to the carriages. In the few minutes it took us to wake up and realise what was going on, the train started to move. All we could think of was we weren't ready. Besides not being dressed, we hadn't stowed things away and we were about to leave the car 200 kilometres behind at the station. In a matter of seconds, my boss decided he would get off and grab the car while I stayed on the train and secured everything. I don't think anyone has ever dressed so quickly, grabbed the car keys and jumped off a moving train. I was impressed. Left on the train, I had time to leisurely get dressed and go through the carriages, securing them before the trip got too rough. It was unplanned but a great journey between the 2 towns on the train that day. Country train rides are a fabulous way to relax and enjoy the countryside.

I don't know whether I should mention this next story as it is a quite embarrassing moment in my career as a science communicator but, hopefully, it's been long enough that time will have made it less awkward.

While working at Sydney Observatory giving tours of the oldest telescope to whoever was in the building at the time, I would explain that it was a refracting telescope, which meant it had a lens at the front of the long tube and a lens at the other end. I would point out each item as I was talking. Occasionally I would mix things up and swing the telescope down to some person in the group and ask them to take off the protective cap at the end. I would then ask what they saw and, hopefully, they would say it was a lens (or at least a piece of glass), leading into my talk about refracting telescopes.

One day I had quite a few people in the group, about 20 or so. Being a large group, I didn't pay attention to who was in it as we walked up to the dome and the telescope, especially since a few people were asking questions along the way. Once we were all in the telescope dome, I started my talk (which, I have to admit, was more like a performance than a simple discussion) and decided for this tour I would get someone to take off the lens cap. I swung the telescope down to a gentleman leaning against the wall with his arms behind his back and asked him to do it. Immediately he said no. Being oblivious to everything at that moment, I said it was easy to do. He said I had the wrong person. Still not taking the hint, I carried on and asked him once again. This time he told me to pick someone else and then brought his arms around from behind his back only for everyone to see that he didn't have any. Both were prosthetics.

Have you ever see a western movie where a stranger walks into the noisy saloon and immediately everyone stops, even the piano player, and there's just silence? Well, that's what it was like in the telescope dome. No one moved. There wasn't a sound except for distant bird calls and the wind blowing around the inside of the dome. It was a pregnant pause that seemed to last forever. Thankfully, one of the other people in the group eventually broke the moment by leaping forward and taking the lens cap off the telescope and I was able to carry on and finish the tour.

I learnt a valuable lesson that day. Always know who you are talking to, especially if you want to involve them in the presentation. I never meant to embarrass the gentleman that day, and I hope he was able to forgive me for the blunder.

Incidentally, that wasn't the only 'saloon' moment I've experienced. The same silence and momentary pause occurred when I walked into a pub in Coober Pedy in South Australia. As I walked from the door to the bar there was only the sound of my footsteps and 2 dozen sets of eyes following me. The moment wasn't broken until the barman asked me what I wanted to drink.

### Adult Education

As part of working at Sydney Observatory, I started to conduct adult education courses in different aspects of astronomy for several different community colleges and continued to run them for the better part of 2 decades. These taught me a lot about presentation skills and gave me the confidence to prepare and conduct talks to quite large groups of people. I was still shy about speaking to groups, but after spending the half-hour beforehand pacing nervously, as soon as I started, I relaxed and enjoyed myself. Hopefully, the people attending did as well.

From presenting the courses and running the evening telescope tours, I learned that people were interested in everything to do with space. Most had never looked through a telescope before, so anything they did see was exciting. Most didn't know much about astronomy and how to get started in the field, and they were hungry to hear someone tell them about it. I found I was best able to get across my sense of excitement and impart information if I treated it as a conversation rather than a lecture. People weren't looking for endless facts and figures. They wanted a relaxed, enjoyable time. Some facts here and there were a bonus and I tried to sneak in the learning without them noticing.

With each adult education course I presented, I would organise a trip out of the city to use a telescope in a dark location. In case the weather didn't cooperate, I tried to hold the viewing near a major attraction, so if it wasn't possible to see the stars, we still had something to do. At the time a friend was working at the Parkes Radiotelescope in the Central West of New South Wales, so for a number of the courses, we would go out to the town of Parkes, have a tour of the telescope, do some stargazing that night then come home the following day. It made for a pleasant weekend away.

The weather was usually kind to us, but on one memorable trip, we were stargazing under crystal clear skies when, after looking at 4 objects, someone pointed out that the clouds were moving in quickly and they had seen lightning. I thought we had just enough time to see a 5th object before the storm arrived when suddenly, it started to rain. Fortunately, I had developed a habit of always having large plastic bags in my kit. Don't ask me why I started this habit, but I'm glad I did. I quickly threw one over the telescope and went to get my van. By the time I backed the van, with its tailgate open to provide some protection, up to the telescope and started to pull it apart, it was bucketing down. Since that night, whenever I go stargazing, I always make sure to have the plastic bags with me just in case. Luckily, they have only rarely been necessary.

**Southern Skies Mobile Observatory**

I loved working at Sydney Observatory, but I could also see a niche it didn't address and hence an opportunity to continue working there while also branching out privately. This involved something Sydney did not have, a planetarium.

While at the Ayers Rock Resort, we often thought we should have had a small planetarium to use on cloudy nights. Back in Sydney, where the weather isn't as good as The Centre, I wanted to do something privately that was astronomical yet weather independent, and a portable planetarium fit the criteria perfectly. A full scale, permanently located planetarium was out of the question. The cost of construction alone was, at the time, astronomical (pun intended). Other people and organisations had tried to raise funds to build one in Sydney, but it was just too expensive. A smaller, portable planetarium though was within financial reach. Being portable meant I could travel to different locations, providing they had a space large enough to accommodate the 5 metre diameter dome, and schools, libraries, shopping centres all jumped at the chance.

I operated the planetarium with my old business partner from Central Australia and between us we had great fun going to different places and conducting planetarium sessions. The biggest problem we had was trying to fit these occasional days into our usual working hours, especially once we started to get more and more requests for us to visit. The other problem we had was having to talk almost non-stop all day. If we visited a school, it usually meant doing 6 sessions in the day so my voice never really got a rest. There were a few days when after a couple of sessions, my voice gave way, and I had to nurse it through the rest of the sessions, barely making it each time.

One day I was at a school with the planetarium when I had one of my more surprising exchanges with young children. At about 190 centimetres tall and solidly built I'm a large man, and for this particular session, I was going to have a group of Year 2 students. I was inside preparing the planetarium for the group when I heard them assembling outside. Since it was a portable planetarium, made out of material and held up by air pressure provided by a fan, we couldn't have a door to get in and out. We had a tunnel instead. The tunnel was also held up by air pressure, so we didn't have to crawl, we could walk through the tunnel, albeit bent over. When I heard the group outside, I started along the tunnel to meet them and begin the session.

The only problem was it never occurred to me before just how small a 7 year old child was. As I got to the entrance of the tunnel and stepped out I straightened up from my hunched over stance to my full height, and immediately one of the children screamed in terror 'IT'S A GIANT!!!' and promptly started to cry and hide behind the teacher. It took the teacher about 10 minutes to calm the child down enough to go inside the planetarium. While that was happening, I decided it was best if I went back inside so when the group saw me again, I was sitting down in the semi-darkness. I will never forget that moment, and ever since then I have been very conscious that, to a small child at least, I can look intimidating … even if I'm not really a giant.

Another memorable moment working for myself in Sydney came in 2001 when my business partner and I provided a stargazing experience for an exclusive business party on an island in the middle of Sydney Harbour. Fort Denison, a famous island situated not far from the Sydney Opera House and the Sydney Harbour Bridge, commands perhaps the best view of the city, from a prime location in the centre of the harbour. During the day it is open to the public, and I had been there a few times before, but this time we would be there at night with a private function.

The first challenge was how to get a large, heavy telescope out to an island. We couldn't use a commercial ferry, so we had to hire a water taxi. That way we could take our time getting the gear on and off the boat, plus we could go out and come back when it suited us. The organisers of the event didn't even blink at the extra cost, and when we got to the island, we knew why. This event was huge. They had imported a full-sized snooker table, an enormous bar and numerous other bits and pieces for entertainment. Our water taxi and overall fee were insignificant to the amount of money being dumped on Fort Denison that night. In hindsight, we regretted not charging more!

Given that we needed an unobstructed view of the sky, we commanded the prime spot on the island, the grassy area on top of the old fort. For the next 5 hours, we felt distinctly underdressed but well and truly welcomed and appreciated. If you ever get a chance to spend an evening on Fort Denison in the middle of Sydney Harbour do it. It is a magical experience.

**Macquarie University**

Never let it be said my business partner and I were lazy. As if what we were already doing wasn't enough, we took on yet another project, running the Macquarie University Observatory. The university had a few small domes on campus that they used for students in their astronomy courses. They wanted to open them to the public, and because we only had work and no social life at this point, we opened the observatory every Friday and Saturday night for a couple of hours, although Sydney's notoriously bad weather made it difficult to take bookings and do extensive advertising for the sessions.

We enjoyed our time there, but it was also clear that we had finally overstretched ourselves. We stuck it out for about a year, but then it was time to move on from Macquarie.

## Drug Testing

I started playing Australian Rules Football when I was 17 years old and the one thing you can count on when playing a sport is that you create lifelong friends. One of those friends from my Aussie Rules days provided me with a casual job that persevered for over 20 years. He was working with the newly created Australian Sports Drug Agency (now called Sport Integrity Australia) and needed casual staff to help with the notification and observation of athletes when they were drug tested.

It was not the most glamorous of jobs, as it required notifying an athlete after they had finished competition and following them around at all times until they were ready to give a urine sample. Once they were, I had to watch them pee into the cup and then sign that I believed they had not tried to cheat when giving the sample. As I said, not glamorous, but it did mean I got to see a lot of different sports from the best seats in the house and get paid for it.

Almost any sport was open to drug testing. I went to Rugby League games and grand finals, Rugby Union internationals, national athletic and swimming competitions, Australian Rules games, boxing tournaments, weightlifting competitions, and even indoor hockey games. Each time, having access to everywhere the athletes went and meeting a lot of my sporting heroes in the process.

As a diehard rugby person, the games I most enjoyed going to were the rugby internationals. Getting the chance to stand inside the Wallabies, All Blacks and Springbok change rooms after a game was worth whatever I had to do as part of my job. Having the opportunity to then talk with some of the legends of the game as they were selected for a drug test was definitely worth every moment.

Of course, sometimes things didn't go smoothly, but my job was to follow the athlete and keep them in sight the whole time to make sure they didn't try to cheat. If I wasn't able to do that, I was supposed to declare that I hadn't done so and the assumption would then be whatever sample they had provided was unusable and we would have to wait for them to give a second one.

Generally, if we tested 4 people at a time, one would go fairly quickly, 2 would take about an hour and the last one would inevitably take about 2 hours to provide a sample. That timeline was fairly standard. However, one time we waited for about 4 hours before one person was able to give a sample and then, somehow, while handling the newly given sample, he accidentally dropped it. Ultimately we were there for 8 hours while we waited for him to give a second one.

Sometimes athletes would try and lose us in the crowds that surround them after the competition, mainly because they were upset about losing and needed someone to take their anger out on. Sometimes team management would try and get us to leave the change rooms altogether. But after we have notified the athlete that they are to be tested, we are not allowed to let them out of our sight, so no matter how much people objected to us being there, we could not leave. Of course, we would always try and be discreet and not get in the way, but we never left.

Other times things just went on with business as usual.

After one particular rugby match, the person I had notified said he wanted to try and give the sample. Generally, it takes them a while to do so as they are dehydrated from the game and need to rehydrate before they can pee. To give him some privacy, we went into the rather large toilet area provided for the athletes at the stadium and he tried. After a while though he realised he couldn't, but then said he needed to do a Number 2 and proceeded to sit on the toilet. Not having had this happen to me before, but thinking I can't leave him alone as I am supposed to watch him until he gives a sample, I tried to discreetly stand there and continue the conversation we were having.

After a while, the team manager came in to see how things were going. He then left but came back shortly with a tub full of icy water and bottles of drink in it. He took the bottles out and put them on the floor and made the player sit there with his feet in the cold water, saying it was guaranteed to make him pee. The coach then came in to see what was happening. Meanwhile, I stood there and had to smile at the scene. Here we were, the coach, the manager, the drug tester all standing in the cubicle with bottles of drink strewn around the floor while the player sat on the toilet with his feet in a tub of cold water. No one was in the least concerned about the odd scene, they were just carrying on like it happened every game. The water didn't work, but he did eventually give the sample.

Perhaps the most concerning notifications I ever had to give was when we tested the Australian Boxing Championships. Throughout the day I notified a number of boxers and every single one of them were in such a daze after the bout that I'm sure they didn't even know I had spoken when notifying them. They would sit down in the change room, I would sit beside them, waiting silently, and after about 20 to 30 minutes you could see some clarity come back into their eyes as they turned to me and asked who I was. I felt so sorry for them as the brain damage sustained from each bout was clearly evident.

**Boarding House Assistant**

Perhaps the biggest regret I have with my life is never having had children. However, having said that, another job gave me more than enough familiarity with raising teenage boys.

Working in a school boarding house requires being a parent to the boys while they are away from home and means dealing with all the growing issues associated with boys between the ages of 13 and 18. As a parent, you only have to go through this phase once for each son you have. Being in charge of a boarding house means you have to go through all the stages, all at once, all the time for anything between 30 and 60 boys at a time. In a lot of ways, it is just like being in the movie Groundhog Day. Just as the boys finally grow up and get to the point where you can have a decent conversation with them, they leave and you get to start all over again. From year to year, the details may change but the fundamental issues with the boys remain the same. Every year I found myself thinking that here we are again, the same issue, just different circumstances.

After 13 years of going through similar issues with hundreds of boys, I realised that it was time to move on. I enjoyed watching the boys grow up and love catching up with them now they are adults, some with children of their own, but I am also glad that I no longer work in the boarding house. Like any parent, it's great to have a child, but eventually, you also like to get through those difficult teenage years and see them become adults.

**Orange, NSW**

After moving to Orange to work in the boarding house, one of the advantages is you then have the opportunity to meet a lot of the parents. This gives you an immediate introduction to a lot of people in your new town. Also, since I had been doing it for quite a few years in Sydney, I started running some adult education courses at the local community college. They didn't require much preparation or effort and I figured it was an easy way to begin getting involved in the community. It turns out that this early involvement with the local community changed things dramatically, so much so that after only a couple of years I had a new, and much larger, project to work on.

Once I got to know the teachers at the school and they got to know me, it wasn't long before one of them introduced me to a parent. He was a geologist by profession but also a keen amateur astronomer. One day we sat down and talked about all things astronomical and during the conversation, he expressed his desire to start an astronomical society in the town. Since he was keen to do the administrative work, I said I'd help with the technical side of things. A single ad in the local newspaper and one month later, we had our first meeting.

The Orange Astronomical Society met every month and did the usual society things, but the beauty of being in a country town is that everybody knows everyone else. That means if you have an idea, someone in the society probably already knows who you need to contact to make it happen.

During some of the meetings, a few members wanted to get carried away and build a large public observatory. From my experience, I knew an observatory on the scale they were imagining would cost a small fortune and not be financially viable, so I suggested a better alternative would be a planetarium. It could run regardless of the weather conditions, and the cost of planetariums had decreased dramatically over the previous 10 years, so it was now a feasible option. It was also something New South Wales lacked at the time, at least on the scale and quality I was suggesting.

There were a few smaller ones around, but none were fully digital. In all of Australia, the only ones at the time comparable to what I proposed were located in Melbourne, Brisbane and Perth. As the society members became more and more enthusiastic about the planetarium idea, we became less and less focused on the society, until we realised we needed to temporarily stop and restart the society once we had a proper location. In other words, once we had the planetarium.

Our vision for a planetarium was to create an educational and tourist facility that would not only complement but also enhance the astronomical heritage of the Central West. To achieve this, we formed the not-for-profit organisation Orange Planetarium Incorporated (OPI). The project slowly grew in size until plans included an 11 metre diameter, 80 seat capacity planetarium, a multiple telescope observatory, a lecture/workshop room, function room, display areas, gift shop and snack bar. Unfortunately, as time went on, the project shrank and morphed and grew and shrank multiple times until we finally settled on a design.

From the very start, the aim was to foster community understanding of astronomy and the sciences while offering a major attraction for visitors and tourists to the region. To better understand what it is we proposed, let's momentarily take a step back and talk about the difference between a planetarium and a public observatory.

A planetarium is similar to a library or museum where the benefits and 'profits' are measured in terms of the educational, cultural enrichment, and economic value offered to a community. It is an indoor facility that uses optical and computer technology to project and simulate stars, planets and other celestial objects onto a domed ceiling. They can range from portable units to modest buildings, to grand architecturally designed facilities, such as the Hayden Planetarium in New York. Programs can operate day and night, independent of weather conditions and in the comfort of cinema-style seating. Initially, planetariums just used optical projectors, but today there are more innovative projection systems. In particular, digital systems that utilise the capabilities of modern computers. The original projectors were only able to project star fields, with additional images provided by slide and video projectors. Today, digital systems can show much more than just star fields and astronomical material, making it possible to present shows on a wide range of different subjects.

Early in the planning stages, we realised that to complement the planetarium the facility should also have a public observatory. A public observatory is any place that allows the public to view the sky through telescopes. It can be a large building with multiple domed rooms or an open area, giving a clear view of the heavens. It can also be located anywhere, irrespective of ambient light.

Of course, if you are going to have a planetarium, you need somewhere to put it and selecting a plot of land was not going to be straightforward. Eventually, after many years of discussions, negotiations and site evaluations, Orange City Council finally granted us a patch of land. Altogether over 17 sites were considered before everyone settled on the current option. One, in particular, was on the top of the local mountain. Someone thought it would be a great idea to have a tourist attraction at close to 1,400 metres. Given I live at 800 metres and it is heavily snowing as I write this, I don't think it would have worked. Trying to get people up a snowy mountain in the middle of winter was a big ask, especially given that the council closes the road whenever it does snow.

The first serious option was at the Orange Botanic Gardens. It offered the best overall outcome in terms of location, ease of access, parking, prominence and complementary to existing facilities. Unfortunately, it turned out it was only the chosen site for a couple of years. We now have a new, final location located in the centre of town.

Now that we had the idea, knew roughly what we wanted and had somewhere to put it, the next thing we needed was a design. As a group of residents, we didn't have the funds to build a planetarium ourselves, so that meant trying to get funds from outside sources. But before we could ask for funds, we needed a design so we knew just how much funds were required. At this point, someone in the group had the brilliant idea of contacting universities that had schools of architecture and asking them if they would like to create designs as part of a student project. Within minutes of sending the emails, we had a response from a university in Sydney saying they thought it was a great idea and would use it as an exercise for their Masters students.

After several visits to Orange and multiple iterations of the designs, we ended up with something I thought was quite good. Shortly afterwards, we had costings, and we were away.

We lobbied hard with local and national businesses, Orange City Council, and the state and federal governments. Everyone we approached agreed it was a great idea, and they fully supported the concept, but someone else had to be first to commit money to the project.

We applied for government grants, but because we weren't a local council, we had no chance. A government official even told us that though the grant guidelines didn't explicitly say we weren't eligible to apply, there was no point in doing so as they would simply ignore our application. This was a bit of a setback, but by then I was getting pretty good at the politics of dealing with governments and organisations.

Eventually, everything paid off as we finally convinced Orange City Council to back the project. The council then wanted to move it to a city block that already housed the local library, art gallery, museum and a theatre. We had no problems with this, as it would create a precinct that would be beneficial for all concerned.

Not long after, the idea was raised that we join with the local Conservatorium of Music who were looking for a new home. Essentially we would be 2 separate entities under the one roof. This arrangement had many advantages, so we jumped at the chance. It meant the cost of the joint facility was higher than for just us, but joint facilities are apparently easier to fund. Of course, the new collaboration also meant new plans and designs, and I think the design we came up with is unique and we are more than happy with it. Recently, Orange City Council has secured the full funding required to build the project and construction is due to start sometime in 2023.

When we first had the idea for a planetarium it never occurred to us that it would take 18 years to get it done. I think if you had asked me back then, I had in my mind a timeline of just 5 years. If it wasn't done by then, we would abandon the idea and find something else to do. The problem was, we really thought it was a good idea and would be a great asset for the town and region. Most people in the region, including councillors and business owners, thought so too. It was convincing council staff that was the difficult part.

So, because everyone we spoke to thought it was a great idea, and still do, we continued past our initial time frame and eventually, our exercise in patience and perseverance paid off.

Sydney Observatory

The Harbour Bridge, looking from between the two large domes at Sydney Observatory

Parkes Radiotelescope

Our portable planetarium, showing the inflated entrance way

The Macquarie University Observatory

Architectural design for the Orange Regional Conservatorium and Planetarium

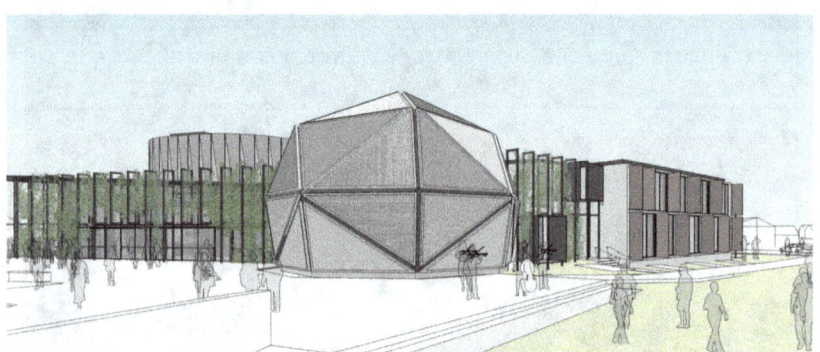

# Part Two
# Life

# CHAPTER 4
# Injuries

---

**Heights**

Although technically not an injury, more a phobia, anyone who knows me even briefly knows I'm afraid of heights. This fear has defined a lot of what I do in my life and still does. So, in a way, it is an injury, as it impacts physically on what I can and can't do.

Most people have a fear of heights to some degree. After all, it serves a useful purpose in keeping you alive when presented with an extremely nerve-wracking height situation. The problem comes when it affects day to day events that don't pose any immediate threat to your survival.

Some of my friends like to make fun of me when I get them to do simple tasks on my behalf, like climb a ladder to clean the gutters on my house. It's not because I'm incapable of cleaning gutters, but because climbing the ladder high enough to get to the gutters causes my acrophobia to kick in. I get it so badly that even while watching a movie on the television, if the action requires someone standing on the edge of a cliff I get faint, my palms go clammy, and I feel an uncomfortable, sinking feeling in my stomach. Sitting in my lounge room, these reactions don't result in anything more than a feeling of dread that quickly passes once the action moves on. In the real world, however, having these reactions can cause dire consequences.

Most of the time I have been able to manage these feelings of dread. When I visited the Grand Canyon I said to myself I hadn't come halfway around the world to look at the canyon from 30 metres back, so I forced myself to go to the edge and look over. At the time it was winter there, and it didn't help that the guard rail only came up to my waist, so I had a mental image of slipping on the ice-covered steps leading to the viewing platform and sliding into the railing only to tumble over and plummet to my death. In order to avoid this totally real scenario, I sat down on the icy steps and went down them one at a time on my backside. When I got to the railing I grabbed it like my life depended on it and slowly stood up. Once up, I forced myself to look over and enjoy the view, all the while never releasing my iron grip on the rail.

A funny thing happens whenever I make myself do this with a lookout. I always end up imagining what it would be like to fall off the cliff and how it would look halfway down. I really think I could do it one day. Maybe it's the physicist in me thinking about Einstein's theory of gravity, but this thought of falling actually brings me a sense of peace.

Once I had my fill of Grand Canyon vistas, it was time to retreat by repeating the process, but in reverse. That's when I discovered the consequence of having a death grip on a cold steel railing for an extended period of time. When I tried to let go I found my hand welded to the rail by the cold and it took quite a bit of effort, and pain, to get it off.

Sometimes a situation will sneak up on me. I once applied for the position of Visitor Centre Manager at the Parkes Radiotelescope. During the interview, we went into the telescope control rooms for a tour and at one point the person showing me around opened a door and told me to follow. The problem was, he was taking me outside the building to go up under the dish itself. Suddenly I found myself on a mesh platform 3 stories off the ground. I didn't get the job and I think it was because I baulked at that point during the interview tour.

Another common source of height related panic attack comes from roads and bridges. Having an attack while driving can be potentially deadly, so I have to employ all sorts of techniques when I encounter situations I can't avoid. These involve anything from controlled breathing to singing in order to distract myself, to slowing down and staring at the road just 3 metres in front of the car. But the thing that works best of all is simple avoidance of the problem.

Things took a really bad turn one time when I encountered the Gateway Bridge in Brisbane for the first, and only, time. I didn't know what it was like, but as soon as I got to the bottom of the bridge I could see it was steep, very high, and for me, terrifying. Unfortunately, at that point, you cannot stop or pull over, as it is a major toll road, so I had to keep going. About halfway up the world started to spin, I felt faint and I knew that if I closed my eyes I would pass out. Somehow I managed to keep going, but as soon as I was able to on the other side, I pulled over and stayed there until I stopped shaking. As I hinted before, I have never been over that bridge since, and never will again. I would much rather drive through the centre of Brisbane than use the freeway because of it.

Since that day with the Gateway Bridge, it doesn't have to be a bridge that gives me a conniption. Roads up or down steep mountainsides that have no vegetation hiding the view will cause the same reaction. When planning a trip, I look at the route I have to take and if the term 'scenic views' is mentioned at any point it is a red flag to not go that way. An example of this is the construction of a 300 metre long bridge hanging out over the side of the mountain between Glen Innes and Tenterfield in NSW. I will now no longer drive that road either.

My latest encounter, however, was with a bridge on the Pacific Highway at a small town called Maclean in NSW. The bridge spans the Clarence River, one of the biggest rivers on coastal NSW.

I hadn't driven up the Pacific Highway for many years and in that period the road had been significantly upgraded for its entire length. Although now boring to drive on, it is a very good road and a huge improvement from what it used to be like. Normally I still wouldn't have been on it, but this particular time I went to visit an old friend in Forster, who I hadn't seen for a lot of years, before heading up north to Queensland.

While at my friends place his wife mentioned that the bridge at Maclean was the biggest she has ever seen. Immediately alarm bells began to ring in my head. Seeing that I was disturbed by this, she tried her best to backpedal by saying you wouldn't even notice you were on a bridge it was so wide and the slope so gentle. Unfortunately, the seed had been planted and the next day all I could think about while driving north was what to do when I got to the bridge.

As I got closer, I had convinced myself to go over it. My thoughts ran along the lines of, if I die because of the bridge, then so be it. That was until I saw the exit sign for the town of Maclean on the river's edge. I took the exit, hoping to find another way across the river, maybe a smaller bridge further towards the coast.

Once I was off the highway I could see the bridge in its full glory. My friend had been correct, it was mammoth. Extremely high above the river and so long that the slope of the bridge would have been reasonably gentle as she said.

After spending about 30 minutes driving up and down the riverside looking for another crossing and then consulting my GPS and maps, I concluded there was no other way across the river unless I wanted to take a 3 hour detour. So, bracing myself to brave the bridge crossing, I followed the sign that pointed to joining the Pacific Highway and turned onto what I thought was the entrance ramp.

However, as I followed the road it curved around and went across the old bridge, ultimately joining the highway 2 kilometres on the other side of the river. The reason I couldn't find another way across and it didn't appear on any maps was because it was literally underneath the new bridge, so the 2 of them appeared as one on all maps. This then raised some questions in my head. Why build it so high? It was in the order of 10 times the height of the old bridge above the water level. Maybe it was so taller boats could gain access further upstream? But then why keep the old bridge which prevented this from happening. And did the designers not realise some people are terrified by unnecessarily high constructions like this? Or did they just not care?

Whatever the reason, I now have a list of places to avoid at all cost: the Gateway Bridge in Brisbane (it is better to go through Mount Ommaney and use the cross-city tunnels), the Maclean Bridge on the Pacific Highway (get off before the bridge at Maclean and use the old bridge across the river), the Mooney Mooney Bridge on the Central Coast (although the negative to a high bridge, it is a long way straight down the mountain to get to the bridge itself), the new bridge that hangs in mid-air on the New England Highway between Glen Innes and Tenterfield, the western approach to Queenstown in Tasmania, Mount Wellington in Hobart, and the southern approach to Mount Hotham in Victoria.

Apart from the mental anguish caused by my acrophobia, I have also had a number of physical accidents and injuries.

**Cuts**

For some reason, I was extremely accident-prone as a young child. I'm in no way uncoordinated, yet for some reason, I could trip over my own feet while walking down a clear, flat road. I still have scars on my knees caused by one such fall to prove it.

It also seemed that if there was one dangerous thing to step on, I'd be the one to do so.

At my 8th birthday party, my parents took me and my friends down to Berowra Waters for a swim. My friends were already in the water and as I walked in I stepped on some broken glass and badly cut my foot. My party lasted about 10 minutes, at least for me, but my friends stayed while I had to go to the hospital. I still have that scar as well.

Another time, we were all playing cricket on the oval at our new primary school and yet I was the one that stepped on the rusty nail and had it go right through my shoe and foot. That one didn't leave a scar, but I did have to have a tetanus shot.

But even before these events, I had an injury that has affected me my entire life.

**Nose**

One day my 2 older brothers and I were playing Piggy in the Middle (also known as Keep Away) on the front lawn of my grandmother's house. I was about 5 years old at the time and my brothers were 11 and 13 years old. As usual, I was in the middle and my brothers were having tremendous fun tormenting me. I was starting to get angry with them and began working out how to try and win by noting any regularities in what they did when throwing the ball. I noticed my eldest brother would occasionally baulk his throw in order to make me jump early, before then throwing it. So, one time, as he balked his throw I did the same with my jump. The problem was he then threw the ball just as I jumped for real and his fist and my face collided, successfully and badly breaking my nose. Ever since that day I have had a lot of problems with my nose and breathing through it.

Doctors couldn't do much about it until I matured, so I was 20 years old before I had an operation to clear the side of my nose that had been permanently blocked up until then. The operation worked but I still have to live with constant problems. When I retold the story decades later to my oldest brother I was disappointed he didn't remember the incident. I know it was a long time ago, but it was a traumatic moment that left a permanent reminder. Ever since then, all I have to do is mention something about my nose in his presence and he apologises profusely yet again ... not that I would deliberately bring up the subject.

More serious injuries also seemed to follow me around.

**Ribs**

At our primary school, there was a low brick wall that separated an area with wooden benches and a quadrangle area, around which the classrooms were located. At the end of one day, when I was in Year 6, a friend grabbed my bag and wouldn't give it back. As I chased him around the grounds he eventually ran among the bench area. At this point, I had almost caught up and as I was about to grab him he leapt over the low wall but dropped my bag just before it.

Since I was so close I didn't have time to react and tripped on my bag, causing me to fall across the edge of the brick wall and break 3 ribs. The pain was excruciating. After a trip to the hospital and a few days off school, I returned extremely sore and tender. It hurt to twist, or cough, or laugh, or to do anything really except sit still and not move.

Each lunchtime there was an ongoing game of cricket played on the oval. Whoever got a batsman out, whether it was bowled, caught, stumped or run out, was the person to then take their place. They would then stay batting until someone got them out. Whoever was batting the day before would start the game batting the following day. And so the game went on. With upwards of 50 people fielding each lunchtime it was rare for anyone to stay in for long.

Since I could no longer play until my ribs healed, I sat under a tree on the edge of the field idly watching everyone else have fun. One day, however, I heard a lot of yelling and looked up to see someone had hit the ball straight towards me. Without having to move a millimetre I caught the ball and was immediately surrounded by people all wanting to know who I was going to nominate to take my turn at batting. I don't think I've ever been so popular since.

**Blue Bottle**

Like most teenagers in Sydney, my friends and I loved the beach. However, although we were less than 20 kilometres as the crow flies from where we lived to a Sydney beach, it was quicker and easier to catch public transport to the beaches on the Central Coast.

One particular day, when we were about 15 years old, a group of us went to the beach like we had a thousand times before. It was sunny, hot and followed a storm a few days earlier. Just before lunch, while I was in the water, I suddenly felt an excruciating pain around my right knee and although I was in waist-deep water, I'm sure I cleared it completely as I jumped.

As I stumbled onto the beach I found that a Blue Bottle (*Physalia utriculus*) had wrapped its tentacles around my leg, hence the pain I was now in. I'd been stung before, but those times were far less painful, probably because I had only brushed against one tentacle. This time I had multiple tentacles wound around my leg, multiple times. Blue Bottles aren't dangerous, but they are painful and this one had given me a really good shock.

After carefully removing the tentacles I went and sat down on the beach. However, I couldn't shake a growing feeling of uncomfortableness in my stomach. After 30 minutes I figured I had better go get some medical attention from the surf lifesavers, but as soon as I got there I went into shock and the next thing I knew, an ambulance arrived. They put me on a stretcher and wheeled me across the sand, drawing a healthy crowd of spectators, and took me off to the local hospital.

Once there, a doctor gave me a shot of morphine to help with the shock. While I was waiting for it to kick in, I kept thinking that none of my friends knew what had happened and where I was.

When the time came to leave the hospital, the staff asked me how I was going to get back to the beach, but since I had been brought in by ambulance and was only wearing swimmers, I had no idea.

As a 15 year old, I was a bit angry with them, as it was clear I was young, confused and had no money on me and they weren't being very helpful. It was too far to walk, so the best solution they could come up with was to call a taxi and hope the driver would accept that I had no money on me, but could pay once I got back to the beach. To his credit, he recognised the predicament I was in and helped me out. It took a lot of trust on his part as I got out of the car and promised I would be back once I got my wallet off the beach.

As I ran to where we all had our belongings, I came across my friends packing up and just about to leave. Their only comment was that they didn't know where I had gone so they were leaving without me and were going to leave my things at the surf club. I was not happy with them. I could have been eaten by a shark and they weren't going to try and find me.

After paying the taxi driver we all went home, but when I told my mother what had happened she was not at all happy with my friends and let them know it.

**Spine**

Perhaps the most serious, and certainly the most life-changing, injury is when I broke my back. It has become the defining event in everything I have done since.

By the time I reached Year 10 at high school, I had been selected for the 1st XV rugby team. I played in the Number 8 position and during one game our scrum was being pushed backwards. Being at the back of the scrum, I decided I would stop that from happening, so pushed with everything I had. All of a sudden, I felt a snap occur in my lower spine. It didn't hurt and everything else seemed fine, so I continued to play the game. Afterwards, my back ached, but like all 16 year old boys, I thought I was invincible so didn't do much about it. I did notice, however, that every game afterwards it was extremely sore and I would have to lie flat on my back for 20 minutes at the end of the game before I could muster the strength to get changed.

This continued after I left high school and played Aussie Rules for a local Sydney team, Pennant Hills. Ultimately, it was a major factor in my decision to stop playing football altogether, even though it was earlier than I would probably have stopped otherwise.

By the time I did stop playing, I knew what was wrong. I had seen a doctor and had x-rays that showed the 2 sections of my L5 vertebra that locked over the S1 vertebra had broken off that day in the scrum. Over time, this then caused the vertebra to slip gradually forward and put pressure on the nerves.

Apart from producing constant numbness down my legs and at times, if I twisted the wrong way, horrendous back pain, it also had the effect of readjusting my pelvis and the rest of my spine to compensate for the slippage. This had the secondary effect of making exercise difficult and consequently compounding things by gaining weight, thereby putting even more stress on my spine.

To say it defined the rest of my life is an understatement. By the time I had surgery to try and alleviate the pain and numbness, my L5 vertebra had slipped forward by 16 millimetres and it was no longer possible to fix the problem, merely to alleviate the symptoms and stop it from getting worse. When the surgery was over my L4, L5 and S1 vertebrae had all been fused, I had 2 titanium rods screwing them together and spacers had been inserted to replace the missing discs that had been worn away. My only problem with the surgery was that I hadn't got it done sooner.

The difference afterwards was immediate. The constant pain and numbness were almost gone and I can now do a lot of things that had become difficult before the surgery.

Of course, the habits of protecting that area of my spine are hard to overcome. I still think of it as being fragile. But in reality, it is probably now the strongest part of my spine, especially with the titanium rods still in there holding things tightly in place. This was put to the test about a year after the surgery.

I was on my friend's farm, chainsawing some wood when the dead tree I was standing on decided to roll after I had cut off a limb. I know the rule is never to use a chainsaw without firm footing, but it was a massive dead tree, with large limbs weighing the main trunk over to one side and the branch I cut off was relatively small. I calculated it would not have any effect on how the tree was lying and I was only about 1 metre off the ground in order to get to the branch.

After it was cut, I turned the saw off and twisted to hand it to a friend before getting down. As I twisted, my redistributed weight must have been just enough to cause the finely balanced tree trunk to roll over. As it rolled I suddenly found myself 2 metres above the ground and falling. I landed hard on the ground and all I could think of was what had I done to my back. As it turns out, nothing. My back was fine. My ribs on the other hand had suffered and ultimately I found out that I had cracked a couple of them.

My back was not the only football-related injury I suffered.

## Ankle

At the age of 20, during one training session with Pennant Hills, I was running and accidentally rolled my ankle in a small depression in the ground. I immediately heard a loud crack (others claimed they could hear it from 20 metres away) and before I hit the ground my foot and ankle had swelled to an enormous size.

It turns out that I had torn all the ligaments on the outside of my left foot. Every doctor I saw very kindly offered the observation that I would have been better off if I had broken the foot. The injury took quite a few years to get over and all through this time it was sore and decidedly weaker than my other ankle. But after 5 years, following one game, I realised it finally didn't hurt anymore. It is still not 100%, but at least it no longer stops me from doing what I want to do.

## Cheek

The other related injury occurred when I was 25 years old and was ultimately the reason I stopped playing football. During one particularly wet and rainy game of Aussie Rules, I was running to take a mark, focussing on the ball in the slippery conditions and not noticing that an opposition player was doing the same thing.

I am assuming he didn't notice me either, as we suddenly crashed into each other, clashing heads. He was shorter than I was, so the top of his head hit me in the right cheekbone. As I stumbled from the collision I noticed he had been knocked unconscious and was lying on the ground about 5 metres away. I was on my knees, feeling definitely the worse for wear and had to go off immediately, spending the remainder of the game lying in the change rooms feeling like my right cheek was now touching my left one. I have never felt such pain since.

The game soon ended and as my friend, who had driven us to the game, came in and asked how I was, all I could say was take me to the hospital. Neither of us got changed and we left immediately, still wet and covered in mud. At the hospital, x-rays were taken and it turns out that I had fractured my cheekbone from the eye socket right across to the other side. Fortunately, the fracture was not depressed, otherwise, I would have gone straight into surgery. As it was, the best course of treatment was to take some painkillers and let it heal on its own.

I didn't get home until late that night, so it wasn't until the next morning when I saw my mother. Her first reaction was about the black eye I now sported. When I told her there was a little more to it than just the bruise, I could see she was over all of these football-related injuries I was racking up, even though she didn't actually say anything along those lines. Even now I can still feel the small lump in my eye socket from where the bone healed.

As it turns out, that injury put me out of action for the rest of the season, and when the next year rolled around I couldn't muster the enthusiasm to deal with my sore back and injured ankle anymore, so I stopped playing football altogether.

## Achilles Tendon

One last injury worth mentioning occurred only recently.

A group of friends and I had organised a 10 day holiday travelling around Tasmania, starting in the first week of January. Just before Christmas, I was in the yard mowing, trimming trees, and generally cleaning up as it would be about 4 weeks before I got another chance to do so. Over summer, that's a long time to let the grass grow without supervision.

Anyway, I guess I must have raked the leaves a little too vigorously as the next day my right Achilles Tendon was very sore, making it difficult to walk. Initially, I thought it was just a strain, so I didn't do anything about it, and if it was worse than a strain, well, finding specialist medical treatment over Christmas was never going to be easy. Still working on the strain theory, I rested it as much as possible for the next week.

There was no way I was missing out on the trip, so I gave it every chance I could to heal. By the time it came to leave though, it wasn't any better, but at this point, I was going to Tasmania regardless.

Anyone who has been to Tasmania will know it is a beautiful place, full of natural beauty and lots to see and do. Unfortunately, almost everything requires a lot of walking. Plus, there are very few flat areas in Tasmania, so almost every scenic location requires walking up and down hills. When you have a sore Achilles Tendon, that means walking very slowly and with great effort. Hobbling around also uses a lot more energy than walking normally, so I was not just sore, but also immensely tired. However, I was not going to let it make me miss anything. I may have cut some individual expeditions short compared to my friends, but I did see and do everything.

As it hadn't improved by the time I got home, I made an appointment with my GP for the following week. When the day arrived, the appointment with him was at 3 pm and he immediately referred me to get an ultrasound done. He even rang them and said I needed it done straight away, so I left him (without paying, as he said I needed to get there as soon as possible and I could pay later) and went to have the ultrasound. While the radiographer was doing the ultrasound she kept saying "How are you still walking?", which I interpreted as not being a particularly positive sign.

Once finished, she went to consult with her boss and when she finally came back, I was told I had an appointment at 5 pm that afternoon with the orthopaedic surgeon, as my Achilles Tendon was completely torn through.

In the space of 2 hours, I had seen the GP, had an ultrasound and was now sitting in the waiting room of the orthopaedic surgeon.

When he finally examined it, he determined that it wasn't completely torn and that given the amount of time since it first happened (about 5 weeks at this stage), there was no point in having a surgical procedure and to just be very careful and let it heal. I didn't feel the need to tell him that I had walked all over Tasmania with it torn.

It took about 12 months for it to heal properly and now I just have a bit of scar tissue to remind me of the injury.

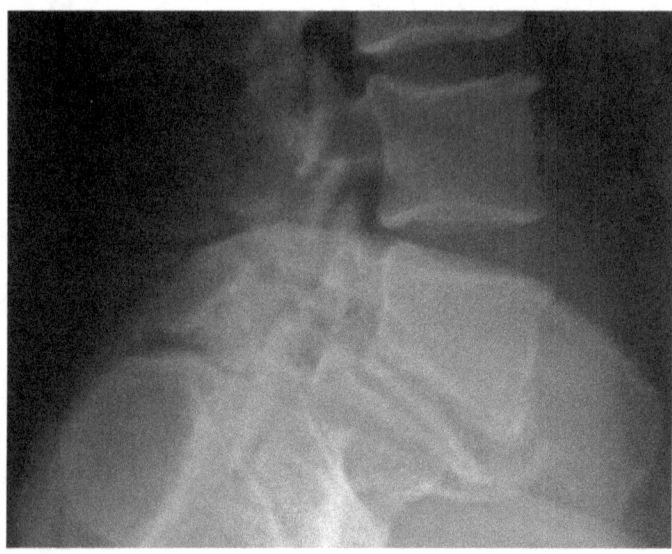

Before surgery: X-ray of my lower spine showing how far the L5 vertebrae has slipped

After surgery: X-ray of my lower spine showing the titanium rods and screws

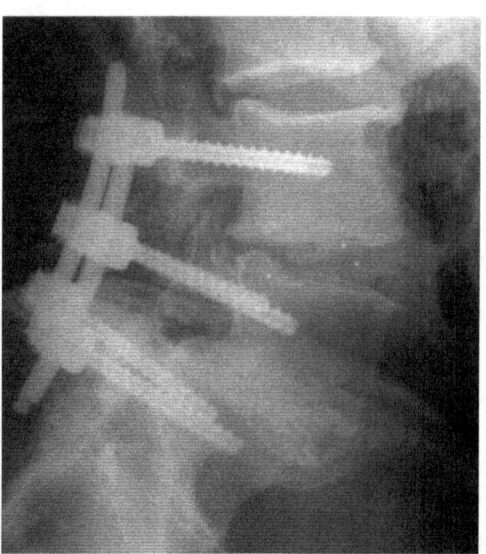

## CHAPTER 5
# Death

—

This chapter doesn't deal with a pleasant topic so I will keep it brief, but having someone close to you die is certainly a huge moment with lasting effects on your life.

By the time I was 30, I felt I had attended a lot of funerals. I know coming from historically large families increases the chances of attending a funeral, but when I sat down and added up all the ones I could remember, I had averaged attending a funeral every 2 years. Admittedly a lot had been relatives that I didn't know all that well and had been taken along by my parents when I was young, and some were acquaintances I only knew casually, but it was still a lot of funerals for someone to attend before they turned 30 years old.

One particularly shocking death was with a basketball teammate.

I didn't know him all that well, but a couple of friends and I had joined a local competition and been put into his team. By this stage, I had finished playing football and my fitness had dropped considerably, so each game I struggled, often having to substitute off to have a rest. In one game, I was off at the time and not really ready to go back on when he signalled that he needed to come off. I was still tired but went back on, only to see him 30 seconds later lean forward and fall onto the court. The game stopped and we rushed over to see if he was okay. Unfortunately, as we found out later, he had died from a massive heart attack. At the time, paramedics were called and they did all they could there on the court for about 30 minutes before taking him away in the ambulance. While all this was happening we just stood there and watched. The incident shook me badly, as I kept thinking that he was fitter than I was. It shook me so badly that I never played basketball again after that night.

Another close person that died was a friend that I had known since I was 5 years old. We had been best friends, although drifted apart as we grew older and went our separate ways. One day, while driving, he had a heart attack. Fortunately, no one else was injured when his car crashed. His death, once again, rocked me, as we were still quite young, and more worryingly, he was my age.

Other funerals I went to were of closer relatives, people more immediately related to me. But the ones that truly affected me were those involving immediate members of my family.

I have already mentioned my grandmother and her house in Turramurra. As she grew older and her health declined, it was obvious that it was no longer possible for her to live in the house by herself. But convincing her to move into an aged care facility was proving difficult for my mother and uncle as she didn't want to go. Eventually, they forced her when she had a fall and had to go into hospital.

Not long after moving into the home, she was once again back in the hospital, this time with a twisted bowel. The doctors told her that if she didn't have surgery, she would die, but she kept saying she didn't want to have the surgery. During one of my visits to see her in the hospital she told me she had lived a good life and it was time. I think at the age of 86 she had essentially had enough of the struggle.

My mother and uncle eventually overrode her wishes and she had the surgery, but the last time I saw her beforehand she was crying and pleaded with me to get them to stop. As a distressed 25 year old seeing my grandmother, who I loved dearly, begging with me, I didn't know what to do. They were the last words I ever spoke to her. The next day she had the surgery but never recovered properly from the anaesthetic. A few days later I visited her and just sat there for an hour holding her hand. The next day she died.

All the relatives were at her funeral, including my immediate family, who, at that point were all spread out. One sister lived overseas, while my other sister and eldest brother lived in northern NSW.

My sister from overseas had come over with her family for the funeral and intended to stay for about 6 weeks afterwards for a bit of a holiday. This turned out to be, sadly, fortunate timing.

About 4 weeks after my grandmother's passing, I was working on a coach tour heading up the Queensland coast. On the first day out of Sydney, we arrived at the campground in Port Macquarie, only to find I had a message waiting for me to call my parents. Fearing the worst, as I figured it must be something serious for them to track me down, I called, only to get the news that my sister, who lived up near my brother in northern NSW, had been killed in a car accident. She failed to take a bend in the road and had crashed into the rock wall, been bounced out of the car, and the car had rolled over her, killing her instantly. One of my young nephews was also in the car at the time but he was fortunately unharmed. My brother had been the one who had to go and identify the body.

Since we would be passing through the region the following day, I stayed with the tour until we got to a town where I was picked up by my parents. I didn't tell the passengers, as I was distraught enough and didn't need them making things more awkward, so I left it up to the other staff to explain why I got off the coach that day.

It turns out that the last time I had seen my sister was at my grandmother's funeral.

Her funeral was quite traumatic for everyone. Following so closely to my grandmother's death, things were already upsetting enough. But my grandmother's funeral had been a cremation and there's something easier to handle about simply walking out and leaving the coffin behind. With my sister's funeral it was a burial, the first I had ever been to, and seeing the coffin lowered into the hole was difficult to watch, for all of us.

A few years later my father retired and my parents moved out of Sydney to live on their land near my brother's property.

It was 5 years after my sister's death and at this stage I was 30 years old and had just started my business at the Ayers Rock Resort in the centre of

Australia. Things were going great, until one morning I woke to the sound of my brother's voice leaving a message on the answering machine. My father's health had never been great, but the last time I visited them on the farm, both mum and dad had seemed fine. The message was talking about how dad was doing okay but he was still in hospital. I leapt out of bed to catch my brother before he hung up as this was the first I had heard that dad wasn't well.

A few days earlier, he had taken ill and been rushed to hospital and mum and my brother were keeping a 24 hour bedside watch with him. I asked how bad it was but I could tell my brother didn't want to say.

Living in Central Australia meant it wasn't a simple exercise to get back to the east coast, especially in a hurry. Nevertheless, I said I would be back if he thought I needed to be. I rang twice a day for the next couple of days and each time I would ask if I needed to be there. Each time my brother avoided answering, but one day I could tell I needed to get over there as soon as I could.

It wasn't easy, organising a last-second seat on a busy flight back to Sydney, then an overnight stay and an early flight to Lismore, where the hospital was located. I intended to go straight to the hospital and see my father, but as I was getting into the taxi at Lismore airport, I realised I didn't know which of the 2 hospitals he was at, so I took a guess and picked the public one. I walked into the reception area and asked the ladies at the desk where my father's room was. At that point, they looked evasive and simply said I needed to call my brother. I rang him, only to be told that dad had died earlier that morning. I had missed seeing him by just a few hours.

Dad's funeral was a few days later and this time it was a cremation. The funeral itself was a public affair, but a couple of days later we held a private family ceremony where we laid his ashes underneath my sister's headstone.

I stayed for about another week, but eventually, I had to get back to the resort, as my business partner had been running everything by himself while I had been gone.

It was dad's death just 5 years after my grandmother and sister's deaths that I think finally drove me into full depression. I wasn't married, so had no one to share my grief with and with the non-stop pressures of running a business, things just spiralled down. I quickly learnt how to hide my grief and depression by smiling and appearing upbeat whenever in the presence of someone else, but it was always just a façade. From that time onwards I had lost all joy. I may have been smiling on the outside, but inside, things were not so cheerful. At least, not until after mum's passing.

Thankfully, since dad's death, I have had to attend only one funeral, my mother's in 2017.

Unlike my grandmother's last few years, mum had decided she was not going to put her children through the same trouble my grandmother had.

The last 10 years of mum's life were filled with major health issues, so she knew it was only a matter of time. She had a knee replacement and then a hip replacement that had to be removed a week later because it developed a bad infection. She was in the hospital for months without a hip until the infection was brought under control and they could put the hip back in. She had open-heart surgery. And lastly, she developed breast cancer and had to undergo painful radiation treatments. All of these after she had turned 75 years old. The cancer manifested in her 80s and she knew that it wouldn't be too long before it finally caught up with her.

Consequently, for the last few years of her life, she calmly went about sorting through her affairs and making sure everyone knew what her wishes were. I spent a lot of time with her making lists on who was to get what of her possessions and going through the old family photos, having her tell me who each of the people were in the pictures. That's when I found out we had photos of my great grandparents. Of course, nothing was to happen until she was gone, but at least we knew and that way it avoided any potential arguments afterwards.

The cancer eventually caused her lungs to fill with fluid. She had them drained, but it was at that point she realised it was only a matter of months to go. Draining the lungs gave her a few months of quality life, but she expressly gave instructions that she was not to have any more procedures, she had been through enough.

It was in these last few months that she realised she couldn't stay at home anymore and so moved into an aged care facility. I visited her a few times in the home but always made sure I rang every day when I couldn't. The last time I saw her I knew it would be the last and so I did something that I hadn't been able to do with my father, I hugged her, said goodbye and told her that I loved her.

A week later I was planning to drive back up and visit her again if I could, as my brother and his family, my sister and her family and my nephews had started to sit with her around the clock. My niece was living in the United States and was coming over and would be there on the Tuesday. I was planning to be there on the following Saturday.

As it turns out, my mother managed to hang in until my niece arrived and even managed to spend all day Wednesday sitting with her and her family. I spoke briefly with her on Thursday but, unfortunately, Friday afternoon mum passed away. My sister and nephew were with her at the end.

Even now it makes me sad thinking about my mother, but I am extremely grateful that we all got to process the grief and say goodbye while she was still alive.

Mum's funeral was emotional, but a fitting tribute to her. For the last time, I think, I saw relatives and old friends that I hadn't seen for a long time and I met her new friends. Like it was with my father, mum's funeral was public, but she was ultimately cremated. Once we had her ashes, we then had a private ceremony at our sister's grave. We interred mum under my sister's headstone with our father.

That night we went back to my brother's farm for a quiet family gathering and the following day a lot of us had to leave and head back home. Before we left though, we would have morning tea at a local café to say goodbye.

We were staying in different places so arrived at different times, my brother and his family being last to arrive. We soon found out why. My sister-in-law's mother was also living in the aged care facility that mum had resided in and during the night had unexpectedly passed away. My brother and his family had to deal with not only mum's passing, but on the day after burying her ashes, they had to deal with my sister-in-law's mother dying as well.

It was a traumatic couple of weeks for all of us.

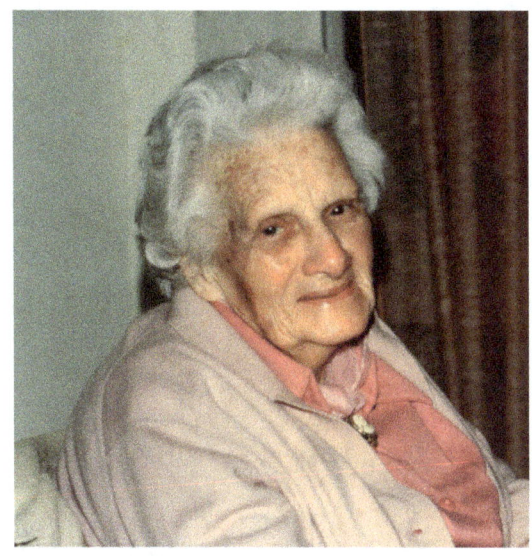

My grandmother, about a year before she died

My younger sister, a few months before she died

My father, 2 years before he died

My maternal great grandparents

My great great grandfather, great grandmother, grandmother and uncle

My mother and me, one month before she died

## CHAPTER 6

# Sport

---

I was fortunate from even a young age to be quite athletic and I found that in virtually every sport I tried I could at least hold my own. The only exception I found was basketball. I was never able to master the art of running down an extremely small court, bouncing a ball and not touch anyone else. It never made any sense to me.

Aside from basketball, every other sport I tried, I loved playing.

The first games I played were of course with my older brothers, although in hindsight I suspect for them it was more a game of seeing how much they could torture their little brother, rather than any recognised sport.

The first organised, community sport I played was at the age of about 8 years old when I played Rugby League, as it was the only winter sport available at the time. Of course, at that age, it isn't the brutal game it is in the older age groups, but it was just as simplistic and didn't really grab my attention, so I only played it for a couple of years.

On the other hand, playing cricket during summer was always something to look forward to and as such, I played it until about the age of 15. At that point, other sports were vying for my attention and I figured it was time to try something new.

**Cricket**

Every aspect of cricket fascinated me and I now realise it was at this age that my obsession with always having to be involved in the action, no matter what sport I was playing, first started. I loved the skill of batting and did everything I could to stay in for as long as possible. Consequently, I would open the batting so I didn't miss out on any potential time at the crease. But, of course, even if you could bat through the innings (which, sadly, I never did) you would miss out on being involved in half the game. In order to avoid this happening, I also became a bowler, usually opening the bowling, and when I was not bowling, I justified having to field as simply being the rest I needed to recover for my next stint at bowling.

It was also while playing cricket that I came to realise I was perhaps more athletic and coordinated than the average person. At times, what I thought was completely natural and just something everyone would have done, seemed to draw comment from coaches and parents. One game, I was fielding in the position of Silly Mid-On, when the batsman did a full-blooded pull shot straight at me. Everyone, including myself, turned to look at where the ball went, naturally assuming it was going to the boundary for 4 runs. Unfortunately, no one could find the ball. After a few seconds of confusion, I realised that I had the ball in my left hand. Apparently, as the ball came at me, I threw out my hand and caught the ball, but because it all happened so fast it was pure reflex and hence taking a few seconds to realise what I had done.

On another occasion, I was fielding at square leg when the ball was hit towards me and the batsmen began to run. I had to run in, pick up the ball and throw at the stumps, but because of the way I picked it up I couldn't throw normally, I had to flick it out of the back of my hand. Not only that, but I was side on to the stumps. The ball hit the stumps and the batsman was run out. To me, at that age, it was just something that needed to be done, so I did it. It never occurred to me that most of my teammates would not have been able to do the same thing.

Of course, I wasn't able to do these sorts of things every time, but over the years they occurred regularly enough in every sport I played to make me realise I was an above-average sportsman. Not great, but at least above average.

My cricketing career came to an end when I was being tempted to try out other sports. However, the impetus to finally give it up came when, in the last game of one year, I managed to have the bowling figures of 5 for 17 runs off 10 overs, yet the entire next season I didn't get to bowl a single over. That sealed it for me and I left cricket forever.

**Rugby Union**

By this stage, I was playing Rugby Union at high school. I began playing in Year 7, but, I have to admit, I never actually learnt the rules during my playing days. I knew the basic ones, but otherwise, I had no idea. I just played until the referee blew his whistle because I had done something wrong.

I would love to have played the game as it is played now, but even so, I enjoyed playing back then, even with breaking my back in a scrum, and even though it was a brutal game in those days.

I played most of my rugby career in the forwards. There was a brief period when my coach realised I was big, fast and strong, so he put me at outside centre for a few games, but I hated it. To me, it was boring. I needed to be in the game the entire time, not just waiting for the ball to occasionally come to me. Consequently, I went back to playing in the Number 8 position and never changed again.

My father rarely came to watch me play. He had a large family to support and a high-level executive position, so he was always working. However, there was one particular day when he took the afternoon off work specifically to come and watch. I knew how big a deal it was, so I was excited to have him there. He was a bit late arriving, which turned out to be a good thing and a bad thing. Good, because on the very first kick-off in the game I caught the ball just as I was hit by 8 opposition forwards. To me, it seemed like only a second, but when I looked up I saw the play was on the other side and about 50 metres up the field. Everyone was in the process of forming a lineout and I can remember thinking, how did everyone get over there? It wasn't the first time I had been knocked out, and certainly wasn't the last, but I was glad my father wasn't there to see it happen.

It was also bad that my father was late because not long after, we had a scrum close to the opposition try line. Playing in the Number 8 position meant I was able to pick the ball up from the scrum and score a try. A few minutes later I noticed my father arrive. Even though he had missed my try, I was really happy to have him there watching the rest of the game.

**Australian Rules Football**

During Year 10, a new student arrived at the high school. He came from Victoria so didn't know anything about rugby, but soon learnt the game. He had to, as it was the only winter sport the school played except for soccer. However, he couldn't completely give up his Victorian ways, so he started playing Australian Rules Football for a local community team, Pennant Hills, on weekends. I soon became good friends with him and for a year he tried to convince me to play Aussie Rules.

By the time we started Year 12, I was beginning to think about what sport I was going to play once I left school. Did I really want to continue playing rugby, or should I try something else? That's when his persistence in nagging finally paid off. I decided to give Aussie Rules a go. Along with 2 other friends, we played our first game that year.

It was the right decision to make. By the end of that year, I was converted to the game and had made so many lifelong friends that there was no chance I would ever leave and go back to playing rugby at a club where I knew no one. I still love watching rugby, but I also now equally love watching Australian Rules.

I played the game for over 8 years, until injuries finally caught up with me, and thoroughly enjoyed every moment. After that first year, where I had to pick up the rules and skills very quickly, I played a lot of my 100 plus games for the club in the highest grade.

There were a lot of memorable moments playing Aussie Rules, as all of them involved my best friends, although, one time, I think I scared one of them.

We were on our way to training one evening and to get there we had to drive down one of the worst roads (at the time) in Sydney, Pennant Hills Road. It was extremely busy, narrow and generally a nightmare at the best of times. It also had a lot of trucks using it. This particular night we were passing a truck located in the curbside lane and I was in the centre lane. I had already passed some trucks in the same way, as did a lot of cars on the road. This particular truck, however, I passed at a bend in the road just as another truck was coming the other way in their centre lane. The problem was this other truck was cutting it very close to the line. That meant as we passed each other on the curve, I had a large truck on either side of me, each only a matter of centimetres away. All I could think of was don't panic, keep the car steady, otherwise, we would have gone under one, if not both, of the trucks.

Anyway, the moment passed, and we continued on, but when we arrived at the ground I had noticed that my friend had been very quiet for the last part of the trip and when I got out of the car my friend didn't, he just sat there. That was when I noticed he was looking quite pale and stunned. I think I scared him with our truck incident.

Perhaps the most memorable game I can remember is when we played our very first grand final. It was an appallingly bad day in terms of the weather. Torrential rain had started early in the morning and continued throughout the entire day. By the time the game was to start, the oval was completely under water and the rain was so heavy you could not see someone standing on the far side of the ground. Nevertheless, the game went ahead and we ran out into the worst conditions imaginable for playing a game of Australian Rules Football.

As I ran onto the field, the water was more than ankle deep and the mud made it difficult to get any traction. As soon as the game began we all found out that trying to mark the ball was impossible as it was so slippery. Trying to kick the ball while standing in ankle-deep water and mud was just as difficult. The game very quickly became one of punching and kicking the ball forward any way you could in the hope that someone else would be able to pick it up and do something useful with it.

Running in mud and water also made it extremely tiring. I don't think I have ever been so exhausted playing a game in my life. At one point I was pushed in the back and fell over. I was so exhausted that I just laid there, face down in the water and didn't have the energy to get up. If it wasn't for a teammate grabbing me by the jumper and pulling me up, I think I would have drowned. Of course, the push in the back incurred a penalty, so after I stood up I had my kick, but because I was so tired and the ball so slippery and the rain so heavy, the best I could do was kick it straight into the defender standing on the mark. To me, that just about summed up the entire game. Even so, I kept going, and when the game was finally over, we had lost, but I was very relieved.

As mentioned earlier, the friends I made playing Aussie Rules became some of my best friends, which meant, apart from playing football together, we also did a lot of other things together.

We often got together to play other sports.

Something we did for quite a few years was play Indoor Cricket, and we had a lot of fun, probably almost as much as going to the club for a few drinks after each game.

## Canoeing

It was during one of these sessions at the club that a friend suggested an activity for us to do next. Apparently, he had always wanted to do something known as the Murray River Canoe Marathon. I had never heard of it before, but, since he was originally from Melbourne and closer to the event, he had.

The race is held every year and is 404 kilometres along the Murray River over 5 days, starting on the 27th of December and finishing on New Year's Eve. The shortest day was a mere 67 kilometres long.

Not knowing what we were getting ourselves in for, we all said yes and we would aim to do it the following year. But before we could show up to the race, we had to buy proper racing canoes and since there were so many of us, we opted not to buy individual kayaks. Instead, we bought 2 man touring Canadian canoes, the racing variety. That way, we could share the cost of the expensive canoes and lightweight racing paddles between the 2 of us, and we could do it as part of a team, rather than individually.

Before we could even think about tackling the Murray River race, we figured we had better do some practice, after all, 404 kilometres is a fair distance to paddle.

We started getting used to the canoes by paddling along the Parramatta River in Sydney's west. This was not ideal, as the river near Parramatta was dirty and smelly, but it was close and we were all able to meet there after work without too much trouble. After our evening paddle, when we took the canoes out of the water, they would be covered in slime that required detergent to get off.

Once we felt comfortable being in the canoe, we enrolled in the NSW Marathon Series of races. These were held all over the state and would give us the much-needed stamina we required. We tried to do all the races that were at least 20 kilometres in length, although one race we eventually did later in the year was 111 kilometres and held overnight.

Most of the races were just exercises in inflicting pain on ourselves. They were tough. Muscles ached from paddling non-stop for 2 hours, bottoms ached from sitting on hard seats for a long time, and blisters came and went.

The hardest we did of these 20 kilometre races occurred at Taree, located on the Manning River in the mid-north coast of NSW. It wasn't the length that caused the problems, it was the weather. As the race started we were paddling into a very strong headwind and the more we paddled the more it seemed we were going nowhere fast. The race involved going 10 kilometres upstream, turning around and coming the 10 kilometres back. We figured if we could at least make it to halfway, once we turned around it would be easy, as the wind would do all the work and we could just cruise home.

The problem was getting to halfway. Due to the conditions, more people pulled out of the race along the way than I had ever seen before. Nevertheless, my partner and I persisted, reaching halfway exhausted and ready to have it easy on the way home. Unfortunately, not long after we turned around the wind dropped and the rain started, making the paddle back almost as hard as the first half.

I sat in the back seat of the canoe, and when we eventually reached the finish line we were both so tired that my partner simply steered the front of the boat into the beach, stood up, threw his paddle onto the ground and walked away. Meanwhile, I was left sticking out in the water without the strength to do anything. Fortunately, our land crew came to the rescue.

While we had been on the water, our land crew had set up our tents, as we were going to camp the night and go home in the morning. But when we all finished and said we just wanted to go and have a lie down to ease the pain, the land crew gave us the next bit of bad news. The wild weather had flooded all the tents and they were not able to be used. Standing in the cold, wet car park beside the river we were not in the mood for news like that, so we all made the snap decision that we would go into town and stay in a motel. It was the best decision we could have made.

Later in the year, in order to step up our endurance, we did the Hawkesbury River Canoe Classic. This was the overnight, extra-long race I mentioned before. Although it was scheduled to coincide with the full moon, so there was some light during the night, paddling in the dark is an eerie experience. In such a long race, the field quickly spreads out, and being dark, it is difficult to see any of the other boats near you. This gives you the feeling of being very much alone. Of course, the organisers take every conceivable safety precaution, having things like lights on each canoe as well as regular safety boats and rest stops along the way, but it is still a long time to be on the water with just your thoughts. By the time you finally reach the end, the Sun is starting to rise and a boat ramp never looked so good.

Having done as many races as we could in preparation, it was eventually time to tackle the Murray River race.

We left home on Boxing Day and travelled to the town where the race was due to begin. After signing in, we had a bit of time to kill, so we wandered around looking at the scale of the event. There were hundreds of canoes, each having associated with it probably an average of 3 to 4 people.

The next day began with a lot of nerves at 6 am. However, once on the water and underway, we quickly settled into our routine and got to work. Each day of the race had set checkpoints where our land crew had to be waiting for us in case we needed to pull in for help or a break. We didn't have to if we felt there was no need, but the crew had to be there anyway, just in case. It turns out that every day my partner and I never felt the need to stop at the first checkpoint, so we kept going, whereas the others did stop. Ultimately, this meant our overall time for the race was a couple of hours faster than the next boat in our group.

At the end of the first day, our shoulder muscles were so sore that we couldn't lift the canoe out of the water and had to rely on our crew to do it for us. Thankfully, the race committee provided a tent where you could go and get a massage at the end of the day if needed and I'm sure we would not have made it without visiting that tent every night.

Each evening, the accommodation was camping at a local oval, and each following morning the day would begin at 6 am with the organisers driving around the outside of the oval blaring the song *Morning Has Broken*, sung by Nana Mouskouri, through loudspeakers attached to a car.

Day 3 was always going to be the hardest. Thankfully, it was also the shortest. Getting up and on the water for the third day in a row was extremely difficult as you were in pain, suffering from lack of sleep because of the constant agony in your shoulders, and you had the prospect that you weren't even halfway yet. However, if you had the mental toughness to get through it, the remaining couple of days were (relatively) easy.

On the morning of Day 3, a friend in one of the other boats woke with a problem in his wrist. Every time he moved it you could hear a loud grating sound. That, however, was not going to stop him. We had done too much leading up to this point for him to stop, so, since he couldn't grip the paddle properly, his solution was to have his hand strapped to it. He finished the race with his hand strapped each day.

When the final day came, we had agreed we would finish the race together, and we did. This meant my partner and I had to slow down to match the others, but when the time came to cross the finish we were all there in a line across the river. Had we not slowed down, I think my partner and I would have beaten the others overall times by more than 2 hours, but I am glad we did. We all started the adventure together and we all finished it together.

With the end of the race being on the 31st there was no question we wouldn't have a New Year's Eve party that night. Since everyone was camping in the same ground, it was impossible not to talk with other people and get to know them. That generated a friendly atmosphere where the entire campground was partying together and not staying in their own little groups. I am glad I was single that night as sex was also rampant among the crowd.

Having completed what we set out to do with canoeing, it was then time to try something else. We continued with the river and paddling theme for a while by going on a number of white water rafting weekends, usually on the Nymboida River, located inland between Coffs Harbour and Grafton in NSW. These were great fun and I don't think there was a single person that didn't fall out of the raft in the middle of a rapid at some stage.

The rafting was great but required a large investment of time and money. Consequently, we only did these trips occasionally. What we needed was an activity we could do together, that was close to home, and didn't require a major effort to organise. Something on a regular basis that wouldn't impact the rest of our daily routines. In other words, another sport.

**Baseball**

We were all at a friend's place one night, throwing around ideas when someone suggested playing baseball. Some of us had played the game before (I'd played for a number of years at high school) and so that was it. Remarkably quickly the decision was made and the discussion changed from what sport to play to what we needed to do in order to play baseball.

There were enough of us that we had a team without needing any outsiders to join, so, a few phone calls later and we were entered as a team in the local competition. We played for a couple of seasons, and like everything else we did together, we had a lot of fun.

The game itself is a great game to play, but the thing that probably irked us most about it was we had all come from a common background of playing football, where if things don't go your way you just get up and keep going and try to do better next time. It was never about demeaning the opposition personally. Unfortunately, with baseball, what we found was the culture seemed to be more about insulting the opposition than playing the game as hard and as fair as you could. This didn't sit well with us. We just played to the best of our abilities, while our opponents wanted to insult us, something we would never think of doing in return. So, after a couple of seasons, it was once again time to move on.

This time, however, we were getting older and people were moving away for work and personal reasons, so it ended up that baseball was the last organised sport we played together.

Of course, that didn't stop us from doing other things as a group.

## Water Skiing

Something we had done each summer for years was go water skiing and that certainly continued. A friend owned a ski boat and his brother owned a property that fronted onto the Hawkesbury River near Windsor, so almost every weekend we could be found skiing from the private beach at the bottom of his brother's place.

We couldn't put the boat into the water from the property, so it usually meant launching from a boat ramp at either Windsor or a nearby caravan park and then driving the boat over to the beach.

On one particular occasion, while we were loading the boat back onto the trailer at the end of the day, a violent windstorm started. The wind itself wasn't a problem and we continued loading the boat, but a nearby shed had an iron roof and somehow the wind ripped off a sheet of iron and sent it hurtling towards us. All I could think of as I watched it coming towards us in slow motion, was that this flying guillotine would decapitate us very easily. We hid behind the boat for protection and fortunately, the iron sheet crashed onto the ground close by, rather than into the boat. Not wanting it to take off again and potentially hurt someone else, we jumped onto the sheet and held it until the wind died down.

Another friend owned a boat that we could also ski behind. It wasn't as powerful so I had to use 2 skis to get up and once out of the water, drop one, but we could use it in other places and not just on the Hawkesbury River.

We decided one day to go skiing with this boat on the Lane Cove River, in the heart of Sydney. We all had a couple of turns and with both of mine, the routine was that after I let go of the rope, the boat would go collect the ski I had dropped before coming back to pick me up from where I was waiting in the water.

At the end of my third ski, I was sitting in the water and could see the boat about 100 metres away looking for the ski. Suddenly, I felt something rough slide across my leg under the water. It wasn't a quick touch like a fish might have done, or a quick nip like an eel, it was a prolonged scrape from something that was obviously big and brushing against me. Immediately, I tried to get all of myself out of the water, not an easy thing to do while you are sitting in the middle of a river. If I couldn't have everything above the water, I was at least going to minimise how much was below the waterline. At the same time, I was yelling to the boat to get back here NOW!

I didn't feel anything else before the boat eventually picked me up, but later, after a bit of research, I found out that the Lane Cove River is a breeding ground for sharks. I really hope it wasn't a shark I felt that day but, unfortunately, I suspect it was. I never went skiing in the Lane Cove River again.

Me, as a very young Australian Rules Football player

In the middle of the action playing Australian Rules Football

Murray River Canoe Marathon finish line, I am in the back of the far boat

White water rafting on the Nymboida River

Waterskiing on the Hawkesbury River

Sometimes ropes just break!

# CHAPTER 7
# Travelling

---

I have no great desire to travel overseas. That's not to say I wouldn't if the opportunity arose, but simply that there is so much to see and experience here in Australia that I have never felt the need to leave the country.

## USA

The only time I ventured outside of Australian borders was when I finished my undergraduate degrees. At the time, my sister was living in California and I figured visiting her was an opportunity I couldn't miss. However, before I got there, I would spend 10 days looking around Hawai'i with my cousin. My sister-in-law's parents lived on the Big Island and they were going to be away on a business trip at the time, so we had use of their place and car while we were visiting.

We mainly toured around the Big Island but did a little sightseeing on O'ahu as well. As I was young and had never been overseas before, everything was an adventure. It was strange to see beaches that had no sand, at least, not like the sand I was used to back home. And to stand on the beach and see snow-capped mountains was completely new. There's nowhere in Australia where that is possible. Plus, volcanoes and lava flows were everywhere.

One of the massive volcanoes on the Big Island is dormant and home to some of the best telescopes in the world. As it turns out, it is also the tallest mountain on the Earth, measured from base to summit. The other is one of the most active volcanoes on the planet.

To see an erupting volcano and flowing lava live is one of the items on my wish list, but, unfortunately, when I was there it hadn't erupted for quite a while. It did, however, allow us to walk into and across the steaming caldera. Not long after I returned to Australia it started erupting and seems to have never stopped ever since. If I had only left my trip for a couple of months, I would have been able to cross that item off the list.

After leaving Hawai'i, my cousin went home and I continued on to San Francisco and my sister.

I was only in the country for 6 weeks, but we packed a lot into the time.

I've already mentioned that I went to the Grand Canyon and had to overcome my fears to look into it, but we also visited some of the other natural icons found in the United States, such as the giant sequoia trees, Death Valley, Yosemite, the Petrified Forest, and Meteor (Barringer) Crater. All of them are spectacular and impressive in their own way.

I particularly wanted to go to Meteor Crater, as it would be the first crater caused by extra-terrestrial means I had seen. Even covered in snow, I was awestruck by the size of the hole in the ground. The other reason I wanted to head out that way is that it would give us a chance to visit Flagstaff, Arizona.

There are so many great stories about intelligent life on Mars. Sadly, most seem to involve the Martians attacking the Earth at some point, so the idea that the red planet could harbour life is not new. We have known for a long time that Mars is the planet most similar to Earth in terms of surface conditions. However, early speculation about Martian life reached a peak when Percival Lowell announced in 1895 that he had (erroneously as it turns out) seen canals on the surface of Mars. According to Lowell, these canals were a final attempt by the dying Martian civilisation to bring water from the polar ice caps to their cities. The telescope and observatory where he made these observations is situated on Mars Hill, just outside the city of Flagstaff. Since I was in the area, I could not pass up the opportunity to visit Lowell's observatory.

The observatory itself is famous for another observation made from there in 1930, the discovery of Pluto by Clyde Tombaugh. During the tour of the observatory I stood outside, looking at the buildings and telescope dome, and thought about how it was here that Pluto was discovered, and Percival Lowell claimed to see canals on Mars. I had a shiver down my spine, and it wasn't entirely from the snow falling around me.

These days we know there are no canals or interplanetary travelling Martians, but maybe at some stage in the past, there might have been life.

On our way back from Flagstaff to California, we crossed the Mojave Desert. I happened to be there at the time the very first Space Shuttle flight was going to take place and it was due to land in the desert about 2 weeks after we drove through. I tried to think of all possible ways I could delay my trip so we could be there to see it land, but, unfortunately, I would be back in Australia when it happened. I always vowed I would go back one day to see the shuttle either take-off or land, but I have now sadly missed that particular opportunity.

Aside from the natural wonders we experienced, we also had to do the obligatory trips to Las Vegas, San Francisco and Los Angeles. Once again, the highlight for me in Los Angeles was astronomical in nature, visiting the Griffith Observatory situated in the hills above the city.

Of course, no visit to Los Angeles is complete without also spending a couple of days at Disneyland.

**Australia**

Once back home from the USA, my friends and I would go on many weekend camping and bike riding trips over the next few years. It allowed us to see a lot of the region within a few hours of Sydney. But where the travel bug really kicked in was when I got to travel further afield.

Back in high school, a teacher organised an ambitious trip that would take us out to South Australia, up through The Centre to Tennant Creek, across to Mount Isa and then back home. It was ambitious because we had just 3 weeks to do a trip that was roughly 8,000 kilometres long, plus any sightseeing we wanted to do along the way. There was little time to slack off, but we made it.

It was also my first real taste of what Australia had to offer.

Aside from the amazing places we visited, one thing that stands out to me now is that at the time, the Ayers Rock Resort didn't exist. That meant we camped in the campground right beside the rock itself. Three years later, the campground was at the centre of a famous incident involving a dingo and today it is part of restricted aboriginal land and not accessible without special permission.

In 1986 I was involved with my first major astronomical event. Halley's Comet had returned, and the world was abuzz with excitement. We all knew Halley's Comet was never going to be as spectacular as it was the last time it had appeared in 1910, but that didn't stop the media from going berserk. It did, however, teach me my first couple of working life media lessons. Firstly, it doesn't matter what you say, the media will edit whatever it is to the point where it is totally out of context. Secondly, they will only use seconds of the interview. To avoid these problems, you need to develop the art of getting your point across in 5 second soundbites.

Even though I knew what to expect from the comet, Halley was my first major comet and I was excited. Halley may not have been as big as some people expected, but it was easily visible from my backyard in a light-polluted suburb of Sydney. I was also fortunate to have the opportunity to see Halley from an extremely dark site.

Because of the Halley hype, a tour company decided to market one of their camping tours to Central Australia explicitly to view the comet. They needed a guide with specialist knowledge to give talks on the comet and the night sky as we travelled around the country. Since the tour company did not have their own experts, they rang work and asked if anyone would be interested. I was the first to put my hand up, so I got to go. It turns out they had such a good response that they ran 2 tours side by side. A friend became the expert on that bus, while I was the expert on mine. We both got a free, 2 week trip to Central Australia showing people the night sky, which we both loved doing. Talk about a great deal!

As a bonus, while we were at the remote South Australian town of Maree (at the southern end of the Birdsville Track), we were treated to a partial solar eclipse.

I had enjoyed the trip to The Centre to observe Halley's Comet so much that I wondered if I wouldn't mind doing this as a job. But as much as I enjoyed the touring, I think it was the opportunity to stargaze from a truly dark place that attracted me. So, as soon as we returned, I applied and got a casual job as a guide travelling all over Australia, which I ended up doing multiple times.

Somehow over the next 2 years, I manage to fit in these trips with my job at the observatory. It wasn't easy, and 2 years of squeezing both jobs in were enough, but I wouldn't change those years one bit as I thoroughly enjoyed every minute. Having seen most of the country, I now appreciate just how blessed we are with natural beauty and how all Australians should see more of their own country before venturing overseas.

I have now been to the most northerly, easterly, westerly and southerly points on mainland Australia. Australia is big (the 6th largest country in the world), so this is no trivial feat.

As part of the coach tours, I visited every state except for Tasmania and the southeast region of Western Australia. Also, since I was only in my mid-twenties, the tours provided me with the chance to have sex all over Australia. I know that isn't necessarily something to brag about, but it does provide extra positive associations with places as I now travel about the country again.

**Queensland**

Heading up the Queensland coast it is impossible not to visit the largest sand island in the world, Fraser Island. With the stunning beauty of its constantly shifting sand dunes, its crystal clear lakes and streams, and its enormous forests, it is a great place to explore. I have been fortunate enough to visit Fraser Island several times and each time I found something new to see and do.

As part of the coach tours, we would stay at a resort on the eastern side of the island. But access was on the western side, so once across from the mainland, we would have to be driven via 4WD troop carriers to the other side by resort staff. The track across was just sand, as there are no developed roads on the island, and it was narrow and wound between the large trees that grow in the centre.

On one particular trip, the resort staff told me they were one person short and I would have to drive one of the troop carriers with passengers across the island. It wasn't a problem, as I had been a number of times before and knew what to expect, at least until I was told the car only had 3rd gear. My first thought was that surely they would give me the best car to drive, considering I wasn't a resort employee. It was quickly followed by the thought, maybe they had and the other cars were even worse!

Anyway, starting off in 3rd gear was quick but manageable. The rest of the trip across was a little more hair-raising. Not having the luxury to slow down on bends meant it was a lot of very quick decisions and tight turns at speed. We eventually made it to the resort without incident, but I don't ever want to do it again.

On the eastern side of the island, the beach is hard sand with small channels cut by water trickling out of the island's centre. It is also about 120 kilometres long, making it the ideal highway for driving the length of the island. However, unlike other Queensland highways, the beach also serves as the runway for planes conducting joy flights. That makes driving along it quite interesting. Apart from no set path, changing water levels caused by tides and waves, and people strolling along the sand, you also have to worry about planes from above.

On each tour to the island, we would, of course, have to have a joy flight. It is an essential part of any trip to Fraser. As the plane takes off up the beach, the pilot has to lift the front wheel slightly as it goes over the numerous water channels. This makes take off a bit of a bumpy ride. But once in the air, the view is spectacular. Often the pilot would let me take the controls and steer the plane around, pointing out where he wanted us to go and then letting me get us there.

When it came time to land, we would have to check to make sure the strip of beach was clear of cars and people and then we would make the approach and land. Usually, everything went to plan. However, one day there was a slight issue. As we were about to touch down, maybe only a few metres off the sand, a trail bike rider came speeding out of the scrub right in front of us. With a good deal of swearing involved, the pilot pulled back on the joystick, lifting the nose of the plane sharply, just enough to get us over the bike, before then correcting and landing the plane immediately in front of the rider. It scared all of us in the plane. I had visions of the propeller chopping up the rider and us then crashing hard into the sand. I can only imagine what the bike rider was thinking. He obviously hadn't seen or heard us and thought it would be good fun to race out onto the open beach, only to find a plane about to land on him.

About 800 kilometres from Fraser Island are the Whitsunday Islands. These are perhaps my favourite tropical islands I have visited so far. The water has bioluminescent Phytoplankton in it, so splash around after dark and the water starts to glow, although, a certain amount of caution needs to be exercised. Depending on the time of year you visit, there can be box jellyfish in the water and these are among the deadliest creatures on the planet. Jellyfish and sharks aside, swimming in the clear, turquoise waters is something not to be missed.

Another must do activity is sailing around the islands. I had done it several times previously with the coach tours and, to me, it was the highlight. But on one occasion I was on the way up to the tip of Cape York with a friend and camping on the mainland rather than on one of the islands. We planned to visit the islands on our way back down, but for that night, we were just using the region as a stopover.

As was our usual routine, we went to the pub that night for a few drinks and found they were holding cane toad races, a typical Queensland thing to do. They would put the toads in the centre of a ring and the first toad to cross the ring would win.

They were selling off the toads in each race to raise money, so people would 'buy' the toads and if your toad won, it would then go into the grand final race. If it won that race, you could win some really good prizes. Unfortunately, if you bought a toad, before the race began you had to pick it up out of its container and give it a kiss in front of everyone, before then putting it down in the centre of the ring.

As we were drinking our beers and watching one race, my friend disappeared for a couple of minutes. I assumed he had gone to the toilet, but a few minutes later, when my name was called as having bought a toad for the next race, I realised I was wrong. He had, in fact, gone and put my name down and I should have realised what he was doing, as he has a history of doing similar things.

Anyway, there was no way out of it as the entire crowd was watching, so I went and picked up what was the biggest toad I have ever seen. It was in a 2 litre plastic ice cream container and there was no space around it, I had to squeeze my hands down the side of the container to get underneath the monster and pick it up. Fighting repulsion at the mere thought, I then quickly kissed the toad and put it in the ring. My friend couldn't stop laughing, but, as it turns out, the toad won and went into the final race.

Having only done it for fun and not expecting anything more, when my toad won in the grand final, we soon found that the prizes were well worth winning. Nearly all of them were tickets for 2 people in various tours around the Whitsundays, obviously donated by the tour operators. Each prize was at least a half-day tour and when added up, we could have spent an entire week there using nothing but our winnings. Unfortunately, we were leaving the following day. Plus, when we came back in a week's time, we had only allowed ourselves 2 days sightseeing and consequently couldn't use all our winnings. But one of the tours we did use on our way back down was a day sailing around the islands. It was one of the best days I have ever had while travelling.

Further up the Queensland coast, just below Cairns, is the wettest town in Australia. Tully has an average annual rainfall of over 4 metres and has the record for the most rainfall in one year for a populated area, about 8 metres, recorded in 1950. However, with an average rainfall of over 8 metres and a highest single year rainfall above 12 metres, the top of the nearby mountain, Mount Bellenden Ker is technically the wettest place in Australia.

Without fail, every time I visited Tully it was raining. The only time it came close to not raining was on one trip. I had spent the last 15 minutes explaining to the passengers that it always rained in Tully, but on that day, as we pulled into town, there wasn't even a light drizzle. That provoked some good-natured digs at me, but trusting my experience, I refused to give in and said it will rain before we left. It started out sunny, but sure enough, just before we left 30 minutes later it started raining. I was bluffing earlier when I said it would rain before leaving, but when it did start, my reputation with the passengers went up significantly.

Not far north of Tully is Cairns, the unofficial capital of Far North Queensland, or FNQ as it is known by the locals.

Cairns is a great place to visit. With easy access to the Great Barrier Reef and tropical rainforests, it is a destination that should be on everyone's bucket list. But I don't know that I could ever live there. as the humidity in FNQ between October and April is brutal.

The first few times I was there in summer it was hot, but it isn't the heat that's oppressive. The problem is the overwhelming humidity that, no matter how much you sweat, doesn't let your body get rid of its excess heat. I would try and have a shower, but if the Sun was up, it was pointless drying yourself. If I had a shower before sunrise I could dry myself, but as the Sun rose I would start sweating from the head down as the Sun slowly got higher. In the end, I decided the best policy was simply to have a shower before sunrise, get dressed while still wet, and not worry about how much I sweated during the day.

You can't visit Cairns without going out to the Great Barrier Reef. It is well worth whatever it costs to get out there and snorkel about the reef with its stunning coral, huge variety of multi-coloured fish, and copious amounts of other marine life. Whatever stories you have heard about how great it is are all true.

But to get out there, you need to take a boat, and that's where some people can come unstuck. I love being on the water, no matter how turbulent it may be. I think the rougher the better and heading out into the open ocean to get to the reef certainly meant that at times the boat ride could be quite rough. Once you were at the reef, things would always settle down, so it was just getting there that was the problem.

I enjoy the ride no matter the conditions, but one time the ocean was particularly rough and the boat was being rocked around more than usual. Most people were inside, sitting in the big catamaran's seating area, as there was a lot of spray coming over the boat due to the rough conditions. A few people were out the back being sick. I was sitting in the very front row of seats but had turned around to talk to a passenger and her teenage son. While we were talking, her son suddenly started to throw up, right in front of me. The mother threw her hands under it to catch as much as she could, thinking it would save having to clean the boat or something. I always figured it was a fairly common occurrence and just assumed they would hose the boat out.

Anyway, the smell didn't bother me and I tried to help the poor lady and her son, but because I was at the front looking towards the back, I could see that as the smell wafted down the rows of seats there was a wave of people getting up and rushing towards the back door, and some simply vomiting where they sat. It wasn't pleasant, but even so, I couldn't help thinking they must have all been just hanging on and it only took one person to start the chain reaction off. In the end, there were more people outside being sick than there was inside the boat. Fortunately, that was the only time I had so many people throwing up on the boat ride.

**Cape York**

As my friend and I continued north of Cairns and into Cape York, we were well aware that crocodiles and other hazardous creatures were to be found everywhere. Snakes and the like were easy, we were used to them. However, crocodiles were a different story as we had never had to deal with them in their natural habitat before. Consequently, we bought a guide, detailing everything we needed to know about the track and camping along it. The number one warning they gave throughout the book was, do NOT go swimming, do NOT camp near a river or creek and do NOT stand at the edge of a river. This seemed to us to be obvious, but also a problem, as we knew there were some rivers we had to cross and only one of them had a bridge at the time. So, when we came to the first river crossing at the Wenlock River, we were confused and a little scared when the guide said to get out and walk across the river first to determine the best way across.

As it was my friend's car, he very graciously nominated me to be the river walker.

Several cars were waiting to cross the river and some of the larger 4WD vehicles were lining up to use a makeshift, and rather dodgy looking, barge that someone had put together. I guess because they didn't want to get their car wet. We had a smaller 4WD but decided we would drive across rather than wait.

The prospect of encountering a crocodile was mitigated by the fact that there was so much activity in the area they would most likely not hang around that stretch of water and as I walked out into the river it quickly became waist deep but no deeper.

I had taken my friends camera with me so I could get a picture of the car mid-stream. Once I had decided on the best way across, I signalled my friend to start into the water and pointed where I wanted him to go. I was still mid-river and as he approached I took the case off the camera, promptly dropping it in the water and watched it rapidly float away, and managed to take a few shots of the car.

As it got closer to me, I noticed the water was over the bonnet of the car and lapping against the windscreen. We had tried to waterproof the inside of the car but I knew my friend must have his feet wet by now. Just as it came past, the car started to lose traction and float towards me. That wasn't good. Apart from the car disappearing downriver, it was going to take me with it. Thankfully, just before it got to me it regained traction and managed to make the rest of the crossing safely. I then finished walking across the river and climbed out the far bank. Fortunately, not a crocodile was to be seen.

Once we moved on, we found the centre of Cape York was, for the most part, a sandy track with millions of non-stop corrugations surrounded by millions of anthills. Some of the anthills easily topped out at over 3 metres high. With so many corrugations it was impossible to travel at any speed unless you wanted your kidneys shaken loose so it was a slow trip.

The very tip of Cape York was exciting to visit and I would love to go back one day, but the best part of the trip was on the way back down when we headed over to the coast to Cooktown and a drive through the Daintree Rainforest.

The main road to the top of the cape goes up the centre, so to get across to the east coast we had to leave the main road and use a less well-maintained track. It was just at the end of the wet season, so we weren't sure if the track was open, but as we got to the turnoff we met a ranger that had just come along it and was going to declare the road open.

The only problem was, the track may have been fine, but the first 50 metres was not. It was pure mud. To drive slowly over it, even with a 4WD, you would very quickly end up being stuck. So, since we were up for a challenge and wanted to drive along the track, we did the only thing we could, we gave ourselves a bit of room and drove as fast as we could until we hit the mud and then slid across. If we didn't make it all the way, at least we would be over a good portion of it before we (probably me again) had to get out and get muddy. Luckily we made it all the way across and didn't have any further problems with getting bogged.

The drive to Cooktown was great and I'm glad we weren't deterred in crossing the mud, however, the best part of the coast trip was the road from Cooktown to Cape Tribulation.

Back in the early 1980s, there were a lot of protests about building a road through the Daintree Rainforest. Unfortunately, despite the best efforts of the protesters, the government managed to start the process and cleared a track. Fortunately, the region was declared a World Heritage Site before they could do it properly, so, because it was done in haste and never completed, the path remains a 4WD track only.

As much as I opposed its construction in the first place, I am glad it was there, as it provided some of the most spectacular scenery I have seen anywhere in Australia. Apart from the magnificent rainforests, in places, you come out of the trees to suddenly see stretched almost immediately below you the crystal blue waters of the Pacific Ocean and the Great Barrier Reef.

Some sections of the track are very steep and narrow. Once you start down the hill there is no stopping. As we sat at the top of one of the hills, building the nerve to start down it, we saw another car come the other way and stop at the bottom. That spurred us on, so we started down, crawling as slowly as we could so we didn't lose traction and slide uncontrolled off the track. After we started down, the car at the bottom decided to start driving up the mountainous hill and that posed a problem. We couldn't stop, and even if we could it was impossible to back up the hill, so we were committed to keep going. But the track was narrow, only one car wide, so we hoped the other car would realise that and stop before they got too far up the track. Unfortunately, they didn't, and when the time came to pass each other we made sure we were the ones on the side of the track where we couldn't fall off the road. It was close, but somehow we managed to squeeze past each other without either car disappearing down the hill.

## Top End

Travel 600 kilometres west of Cairns and you find the bottom of the Gulf of Carpentaria. Wading into the waters of the gulf, the thing that struck me most was just how warm the water was. It was like being in a warm bath.

Heading 400 kilometres south from the gulf and you find the towns of Cloncurry and Mount Isa. Apart from being a huge mining town, Mount Isa is on the eastern edge of some of the flattest country to be found in Australia, the Barkley Tablelands.

The only road west from Mount Isa passes through the tablelands and eventually takes you to the Stuart Highway, the road in the centre of the country that runs from Adelaide to Darwin. As you pass through the tablelands, it is not unusual to notice that for hours at a time the only thing to break the flat horizon is maybe the occasional cattle in the distance. I've travelled the highway a few times and still find it fascinating.

On one of the coach tours, we had to do a bush camp about halfway between the Stuart Highway in the Northern Territory and the Queensland border. These bush camps were normally the times I would try and convince the passengers to sleep outside, rather than in their tent. Since most passengers were either from the city or overseas, it was perhaps the only chance they would ever get to sleep under the stars with a truly dark night sky.

On this particular occasion, it took more than the usual amount of convincing to get people to join me and sleep outside. Their main concerns were with dingoes. Even though we hadn't seen any and even though I told them that dingoes were not vicious or aggressive animals, they still had their reservations.

The most hesitant were 2 girls from Europe, but eventually, I managed to convince about 15 people, including the 2 girls, to join me and we went to sleep looking at the magnificent southern night sky. I did, however, have to agree to let them sleep in the middle of the group and that I would be on the outside. I didn't have the heart to tell them that dingoes weren't the problem and that they should be more concerned about snakes and scorpions.

Anyway, in the middle of the night, we were all woken by the loud screaming of one of the European girls. As everyone sat up quickly, suddenly fully awake, we could see that a dingo was tugging at her blanket, trying to drag it off her, but as soon as it realised there was activity, it let go and ran off. Amazingly, it had walked past me and half a dozen other sleeping people to pick on the one person in the group who was the most concerned about dingoes.

Needless to say, there was a flurry of tents being erected in the early hours of the morning and when everyone finally went back to sleep, there was just me and 2 others who remained under the stars.

## Time Zones

Travelling across state borders can bring about some confusion with times if you are not aware of the changes. Australia has 3 time zones. Queensland, New South Wales, Victoria and Tasmania are all 10 hours ahead of Greenwich Mean Time. South Australia and the Northern Territory are 9½ hours, while Western Australia is 8 hours ahead. From a purely geographical standpoint, the central states should really be 9 hours and not 9½, but early on, political reasons caused them to decide to be only half an hour behind the eastern states. When you throw in that some states adopt daylight saving times for half of the year, and others don't, things can get confusing, especially if you keep crossing state borders in rapid succession.

On one trip we were travelling from Tibooburra in the northwest corner of NSW, to Innaminka in the northeast corner of South Australia, to Birdsville in the southwest corner of Queensland. Innaminka being famous for where the ill-fated expedition of the explorers Burke and Wills ended.

We were travelling from Tibooburra to Birdsville in one day, stopping at Innaminka for lunch, and that meant crossing a number of state borders in swift sequence. At the time, NSW was on daylight saving time but Queensland and South Australia were not.

So, in order to get to our destinations, the road left Tibooburra and crossed into Queensland, which meant setting our watches back one hour. It then went into South Australia, which required turning our watches back a further half an hour before then passing back into Queensland, so the watches had to go forward again by half an hour. All of this occurred with a few hours. It was very confusing.

**South Australia**

South Australia is the driest state in the country and is primarily desert. But, it also has some of the most spectacular scenery and interesting locations to visit.

One if my favourite spots in the country is the Flinders Ranges. If you have never been then shame on you! It is well worth it. In a word, the area is stunning, awesome, magnificent and spectacular. Within the Flinders Ranges, stunning red rock hills create a natural bowl known as Wilpena Pound. It is outstanding and well worth a visit.

The road from Blinman to Parachilna passes through an ancient landscape with vertical folded rock layers and spectacular scenery. At one point along the road you come over a rise to leave the ranges behind and see the wide flat expanse of the red centre stretching out in front.

When visiting the outback, some people just see a wide expanse of nothing. But I see, and feel, a land of power and stunning beauty that tolerates us mere humans as we run around on its surface. Those that also feel this way have a chance of surviving. Those that fall into the first category had better beware. I love this sort of country. Open, majestic, and filled with a sense of untamed serenity.

The Oodnadatta Track has artesian wells dotted along its length that you can swim in. And one the best aspects of travelling along outback roads is that if you stop along the way you are immediately struck by the exhilarating embrace of deafening silence. No birds, no flies, no wind, just your breathing making the only sound.

Lake Eyre is the largest lake in Australia, although it rarely completely fills with water, so is mainly a giant salt lake. I have been there about a dozen times now and have been extremely fortunate to see it filled with water on 3 of those occasions. It usually requires heavy rains and flooding in Queensland in order to have the water trickle down through the Channel Country and into the lake.

And towns like Woomera and Coober Pedy have so much history you have to spend more than a casual bit of time in them.

Woomera was the site of Australia's space program. The town itself is where the people who worked at the launch facility lived, but, unfortunately, when the facility closed down, the majority of people left. The town was run down apart from a central area for a while, but these days it is a thriving, if not overly vibrant, town. The facility itself still has the old launch pads and has lately been used for space-related activities once again.

Coober Pedy is where the vast majority of the world's opals come from. It is a hot, dusty, and not a very pretty place, BUT, it is extremely interesting. I have been there a few times and always found the underground houses and opals well worth the visit, however, it wasn't until we did a sightseeing flight over the region that I realised just how beautiful the area is.

The opal mines are essentially holes a few metres across drilled straight down into the ground, with the rubble excavated from the hole put into a pile off to one side. Around the town itself, the mining leases aren't very big in area, so from the air, you can see that there are holes and their associated rubble everywhere. Thousands of them. The rubble exposes the many colours of the ground and gives the entire region the effect of being a giant, multi-coloured impressionistic painting.

One aspect of Coober Pedy that made you realise just how difficult living there could be was the water. I guess the reason that makes it such a great place for opals to form also makes the water extracted from the ground extremely hard. The mineral content of the water from the Great Artesian Basin makes it impossible to drink without purification, and that makes all fresh water in the town an extremely valuable commodity. Consequently, the water used for showers provided to tourists was not purified, simply the water straight out of the ground. With so many minerals in it, this made using soap virtually impossible. The only way I found to get a lather, and hence clean myself was to use shampoo instead of the standard cake of soap. Plus, you had to do it quickly, as the showers were all timed to providing just a few minutes worth of water.

The Breakaways, outside of Coober Pedy, are a great place and the site where such cinematic classics as *Mad Max: Beyond Thunderdome* and my favourite Vin Diesel movie *Pitch Black* were made. The spacecraft they used in the movie is still located in town but sadly hasn't survived the terrestrial weather at all well over the last 20 years.

## Western Australia

Western Australia is big. Very big. If it was a country it would easily be the 10th largest in the world by area. Which is why there is so much to see and do in the state.

The only region I have been to twice in Western Australia is the Kimberley region in the north. A land of Boab trees, and striking escarpments, towns such as Kununurra, Halls Creek and Broome, plus places like Lake Argyle and The Bungle Bungles, all highlight not just the stunning beauty of the region, but also its incredible remoteness. Unfortunately, I haven't been able to visit the Bungles Bungles on the ground, but I have managed a scenic flight over them. The word spectacular does not do them any justice and it is on my bucket list to eventually get back there and spend some time exploring in more detail.

From the town of Halls Creek, there is a track that cuts across the country to Alice Springs in the Northern Territory, the Tanami Track. It is difficult to imagine anywhere as remote as you find yourself while travelling its length.

Apart from a major gold mine about halfway, the other, and I think far more interesting, attraction is the large meteorite impact crater of Wolfe Creek. Located about 130 kilometres from Halls Creek, the crater is at the end of an access road that has so many corrugations it rattles your teeth loose if you drive any faster than 5 kilometres per hour.

Like the crater in the United States I had seen years earlier, Wolfe Creek is relatively young and so still has the distinct shape of a hole in the ground. It is a bit older, so the inside has filled in a bit, but even so, it looks like the image everyone has of a massive crater caused by a rock from space crashing into the ground at speed. There are larger meteorite craters in Australia, but none are as clearly formed as this one. Brilliant, impressive, extraordinary, are all pale adjectives for the magnificence that is the crater and I could have spent a lot longer exploring it and the surrounding area but, unfortunately, I had to keep moving as there was still a lot of kilometres to go before I reached anywhere.

At the other end of the Tanami Track, around the Alice Springs region, there are some more meteorite craters, bringing the total I have now visited to 15, although, to be fair, 12 of them are in the one place.

Gosses Bluff is an old, eroded crater about 22 kilometres across, while the Henbury Meteorite Craters are a group of 12 that were formed when the meteor broke apart in the atmosphere and the individual fragments crashed into the ground. The largest in the group is about 180 metres across.

I've had a lot of people say to me that they're not interested in travelling in the outback because it's just flat desert and nothing to see. The reality is very different to this assumed summation. There is indeed a lot of desert, and there aren't many mountain ranges, but that doesn't make it uninteresting.

Broome is the capital of the Kimberley region and an extraordinarily clean and tidy town. They obviously take their tourism seriously and keep it looking good.

One of the big tourism drawcards they tout are some supposed dinosaur footprints in the rocks around the local headland. However, after spending an hour and a half first thing one morning looking for them, along with a family doing the same thing, I was not so sure. eventually we agreed that a few possibilities were in fact real dinosaur footprints, although others may dispute our findings.

After leaving clean, tidy, and nice Broome, the next town was not so pleasant. Port Hedland turns out to be the poster child for how to fuck up a huge region, completely, and not give a shit that everyone knows it was you who did it. There are major highway roads into and around town that major cities would be envious of. However, EVERYTHING in the town is covered with red dust: the cars, shops, signs, railings, trucks, the road ... everything. Unlike Broome, which embraced tourists, Port Hedland is obviously nothing but a mining port and anyone who isn't a miner is just in the way. The best part of Port Hedland was the scenery of the Great Sandy Desert on the way there.

When heading south from Port Hedland, it isn't long before the land once again becomes nice. Although, the sand and rocks take on a dark, blood red colour, obviously displaying its heavy concentration of iron. The land itself has an ancient, weary feel about it. It is old (some of the oldest landscape on the earth) and feels like it has slumped under the weight of its age. It is flat and the occasional hill is crumbling as it tires from the effort to resist time. In other words, it is totally awesome!

Continuing south is the small town of Exmouth. Along the way Sturt Desert Peas line the side of the highway and the water of the Indian ocean is nothing short of the most spectacular blue. Exmouth is also the place where you are able to swim with the largest fish in the sea, the whale shark. I always enjoy being on water but the day I did the whale shark swim is one of the best days I have ever experienced. I had 2 swims with a 7 metre long whale shark (not as huge as they get, but not small either), a couple of snorkels around the reef looking at the fish swimming about the coral, and lots of humpback whales frolicking not far from the boat. With full sunshine, warm temperature and not a cloud in the sky, I would categorise it as a perfect day.

A fair way south of Exmouth is a little town called Kalbarri, outside of which is my new favourite national park. The Western Australian wildflower season had just started when I was there and the park was stunning. But the main reason for visiting the park was to go to the spectacular Kalbarri Skywalk. Two cantilevered, see-through platforms hung out by around 100 metres over a deep gorge. It was the first time I had to test the limits of my height phobia for a long time and I was determined to walk out and look at the view. I am so glad I did, as the view was stunning, and because I stayed out there for quite a while my phobia began to ease.

Located east of Pemberton, near the start of the Great Australian Bight, is the realm of the big Karri trees. The trees are well worth a visit just to see them from the ground, but at the Valley of the Giants Treetop Walk they are truly spectacular. The treetop walk is just that, a series of raised catwalks meandering its way through the upper levels of a large grove of Karri trees. Even though at one point it was 40 metres above the ground, I was able to do it thanks to my new found confidence to conquer heights, although, there were moments when my old anxiety desperately wanted to come to the surface. But, I did it and I am so glad I did.

North of the big trees is another spectacular natural feature known as Wave Rock. Walking under, over and around Wave Rock all I can say is wow. Not just the wave, but the total rock outcrop including the Hippo's Mouth formation. Just, wow.

Continue heading east and eventually you hit the Nullabor. I have to admit that the Western Australian side of the Nullabor is a bit disappointing. At least for me. I had visions of a flat, vegetation free plain that stretches for a thousand kilometres. The opposite is true until you hit the border. There were lots of trees and shrubs. Given that the name Nullabor literally means "no trees" I was disappointed. However, the first interesting road stop you encounter is Balladonia, the site where the US space station Skylab fell to Earth in 1979 and scattered over the countryside.

Not long after leaving Balladonia is the longest straight stretch of road in Australia. At 146.6 km long it is certainly long but passes remarkably quickly. Interestingly, that whole region from Balladonia to the town of Eucla on the border, have the weirdest idea about time zones. Although not an official Australian time zone, they insist they are 45 minutes ahead of the rest of Western Australia and hence only 45 minutes behind South Australia. There are signs and clocks everywhere constantly reminding you of this.

If I had been disappointed with the Western Australian stretch of the Nullabor, the South Australian stretch from Eucla to Nullabor was exactly what I thought it should be. It includes the spectacular Bunda Cliffs and the beautiful Head of the Bight Whale Sanctuary. I spent an hour at the sanctuary watching a southern right whale and her 2 babies frolicking literally just metres from the shore.

## Northern Territory

Between Darwin and Alice Springs there are world-class, natural attractions everywhere. Kakadu and Litchfield National Parks are prize examples. Katherine Gorge, The Devil's Marbles, and Mataranka hot springs are some more.

I will never forget the first time I went to Mataranka. We arrived there late and by the time we had set up camp, had dinner and cleaned up, it was about midnight. It had been a long day and although I was tired I felt I needed to relax before going to bed. I headed over to the hot springs, which are a soothing 34 degrees all year round, mercifully crocodile free, and immersed myself into the warm water. The only light around was the full Moon and even though I was in water up to my chin, about 180 centimetres deep, the water was so clear that I was able to see the hairs on my toes. I think I could have slept in the water overnight it was so relaxing, but sadly, after an hour I thought I had better get out in order to get some sleep, ready for the following day. However, every time I have been back since, I always make sure to factor in more time to enjoy the springs.

Incidentally, just south of The Devil's Marbles is the small roadhouse of Wycliffe Well. There's nothing of particular note about it except that it claims to be the UFO capital of Australia. I have yet to be convinced. There were some strange people exiting metal machines, but it turns out they were just people in caravans. No aliens unfortunately.

Another gem to be experienced is the Simpson Desert. Encompassing parts of the Northern Territory, South Australia and Queensland, it is made up of fine, brilliant red sand dunes. The colour is not dull, as a lot of people assume, but is bordering on being fire truck red, making sunrises and sunsets extra special as it looks like the sand is on fire. Close to the western edge of the desert is Dalhousie Springs, a series of large pools where the waters of the artesian basin come to the surface. Like every other spring you come across in the deserts of Australia, you have to swim in the Dalhousie pools.

On the eastern side of the Simpson Desert is the famous town of Birdsville. I always wondered why it was called that until I visited it for the first time and found that there are thousands and thousands and thousands of birds in the district. Massive flocks of budgerigars were everywhere, only just out-doing the flocks of galahs. Crows constantly maintain their distinctive call throughout the day and collectively, the menagerie of birds was never going to let you sleep past the first rays of sunrise.

Unfortunately, when we arrived on that first trip it was late in the afternoon and things were relatively quiet, so some of the passengers set up their tents under the few trees in the campground. The following morning we realised this was not a great idea, as they were covered in copious amounts of bird poop.

Not many people permanently live in Birdsville but they do get a lot of tourists visiting, especially when the Birdsville races are on. I've been in the town when essentially we are the only non-residents there, coming close to doubling the town's population. And I've also been there during the races, when the town is swamped by over 5,000 people, arriving by any means possible. It's not unusual to see people arriving by private planes, buses, cars, and horses.

Even with such high tourist visitations, there is still only one pub in the town and on that first trip, we all had to have a beer in the famous Birdsville pub. But when we entered, the publican gave us the spiel about how we could have any beer we liked, as long as it was a XXXX beer. Thinking this was just a bad attempt at humour, given we were in Queensland, I smiled until I looked in the fridges behind the bar. Sure enough, the only beer in there was XXXX. I don't know whether it was just a case of a momentary shortage of other brands, or waiting for a delivery, or whether that was all they ever had, but thankfully, in subsequent visits, they had at least a few more varieties to choose from.

I think the coldest I have ever been while travelling around the country occurred while camping along the Birdsville Track. We had left the town of Marree in South Australia, heading to Birdsville, but stopping halfway for a bush camp. As was my usual routine, I didn't use a tent and just threw my sleeping bag on the ground outside. I'm not against tents, just that when you are in the middle of nowhere and there are no artificial lights for hundreds of kilometres and the sky is clear, in my opinion, it is a crime not to fall asleep while looking at the magnificent night sky.

The problem was, even though we were in the desert and at about the same latitude as Brisbane, it was winter, and desert nights can get very cold at that time of year. Normally, it wasn't an issue, as I had a nice warm sleeping bag, but this time I literally did fall asleep while looking at the stars, so my head was exposed outside of the bag. I remember half waking up a few times in the night and thinking my head was cold and trying to snuggle into the sleeping bag a bit further, but I could never get warm enough and certainly could never get back to sleep properly. Eventually, at around 4 am, I thought I might as well get up, as I was cold and sleep was never going to happen. That's when I sat up and in doing so, the sheet of ice that had formed on my face and head cracked and fell off. No wonder I was cold.

It took me a while sitting in front of a small fire I made, but eventually, I managed to warm up.

## The Centre

Alice Springs is not a capital city, although it probably should be. It is, however, the unofficial capital of Central Australia. Located almost in the exact centre of the continent, it is 1,500 kilometres from the nearest city and consequently a vital town for a large portion of inland Australia.

There is a good reason the town was originally located where it was, in particular, it had a permanent source of water and like most places around the country, there is a lot of natural beauty close by.

Since I am not a geologist, one of the things that always intrigued me was located just outside of town, the Finke River. Apparently, it is the oldest riverbed in the world with parts of it dated to about 350 million years old. How they determined that is beyond me as a simple physicist, and even though it is dry for most of the time, it does occasionally rain and the river will have water in it. Given the surrounding area is purely sand, I don't know how it could not change over time, or even disappear completely, even if it only fills every so often.

Also, just south of town and visible from the highway, are the domes of the secret American base, Pine Gap. Every time I drove past them I would wonder what it was like in there and exactly what they did. I mentioned this to the driver one time and the next thing I knew, we had turned off the highway and were heading for the base. When we arrived at the gates, a very stern-looking soldier carrying a gun stood in the middle of the road and without a smile or simple hello said "Turn around now". Given he looked like he meant business, we turned around and left. The disappointing thing was that at no point once we left the highway could we see the base or the domes. It turns out, the best view is from the main road into town.

Every year Alice Springs holds events unique to the town. Perhaps the strangest one being the Henley-on-Todd boat race. Held in the dry riverbed of the Todd River that runs through the city, it is maybe the only boat race in the world that is cancelled when there is actually water in the river. I haven't competed in the races but I have been to a few and the carnivals are the best fun you can have in just one day. I have, however, competed in another race day held at Alice, the Camel Cup.

Camels are not the easiest animals to ride. They tend to have a belligerent nature and do whatever they want, rather than follow your instructions.

As part of the tour out to The Centre, we would always stop at the Alice Springs Camel Farm so the passengers could have a ride on a camel. One particular trip coincided with the running of the Camel Cup the following day and since we were in town for a few days it was an opportunity not to miss. Especially since the owners of the camel farm were organising a novelty race where the jockeys would be the staff from all the coach tours in town at the time, and that meant me. It was great fun, if just a little bit scary.

Even though I had ridden horses before, that meant nothing when trying to control a camel. Initially, when the race began, I couldn't get the animal I was on to start running and then, all of a sudden, it decided to run. I could see people were on camels running the wrong way, so apparently I wasn't the only one having issues. Riding a camel is not the most comfortable thing to do and when they are running at speed, even less so. But eventually, the race ended and everyone thought it was a great spectacle. I have to admit it was fun but there were also moments of terror thrown in there, so I was glad when it was over.

In the Western Macdonnell Ranges outside of Alice Springs there are a number of water holes. Even though it is in the middle of the outback, when I went for a swim in one of them, Ellery Creek Big Hole, the water was cold. So much so that it took my breathe away and I could only manage to stay in for a couple of minutes. I think the Tumut River in the Snowy Mountains of NSW is still the coldest place I've ever swum, but this comes a close second!

Heading south-west and about halfway between Alice Springs and Uluru is Kings Canyon, a massive cleft in some sandstone hills caused by a creek that occasionally flows. Looking like a giant V-shaped wedge, the sides of the canyon are sheer and high. The main walk involves a steep climb on one side of the canyon opening to get up to the rim and then following the edge of the canyon around to eventually descend on the other side 6 kilometres later. While up on the rim there is very little protection from the harsh desert sun, so it can get dangerous if you are not prepared. Although I've done the walk a dozen times, I never get tired of it and the view, but on one trip I thought it was a bit too dangerous to do the climb and consequently made the decision that the group would not walk around the rim.

As we arrived in the car park and got out of the bus, we discovered the outside temperature was 46 degrees Celsius. This is extremely hot and the prospect of doing a 6 kilometre walk in full sun in that temperature was potentially deadly. Rather than expose ourselves to these conditions, we decided a safer walk would be to go along the riverbed at the bottom of the canyon.

There were a lot of trees providing some shade and it was a much shorter walk, so we figured that way we could still experience the canyon without subjecting ourselves to life-threatening heat conditions.

The riverbed turned out to be a difficult trip as well, but at least it was relatively short. The path was strewn with giant boulders, obviously cleaved off the canyon walls, that required climbing over with the assistance of everyone else, kind of like a giant obstacle course, and by the time we got to the end, at the point of the V shape, we were hot and tired.

At the very end, directly under where the water would cascade off the rim of the canyon, there was a small pool of water. Given the temperature, it was far too enticing not to splash some of it onto ourselves, so I laid down on a flat rock extending into the pool, dipped my head in the water and then filled my hat and poured some water over my body. Since the rock was very hot, I got up quickly and turned around, only to find the others pointing and telling me to move. I jumped off the rock, not knowing what was going on, but when I turned I could see a snake slithering over where I had just been. I must have disturbed it when I put my head in the water and it followed me out as I stood up.

The snake had a yellow and brown stripe pattern and was about 1½ metres long. After I was back in Sydney I did some research and I think it was a Woma, a water python. They're thankfully non-venomous, but I still wouldn't like to have one bite me on the face while wetting my head in a pool of water, especially in the middle of Australia, hundreds of kilometres from the nearest hospital.

I recently went back to Central Australia and Kings Canyon. The walk along the bottom is now a lot easier, with boardwalks and viewing platforms, although it is no longer possible to get all the way to the end anymore.

Once back at the bus and ready to leave, I did the usual headcount and discovered I was one passenger short, a European tourist. Concerned for his safety, I did a quick scout around the area and finally located him walking along the rim of the canyon. Against our decision and all common sense regarding the excruciatingly hot conditions, he had decided to climb the rim and walk in the unprotected heat without telling anyone what he was doing. Apart from the recklessness in doing so, it turns out he only took a litre of water with him. He was lucky he didn't die from dehydration and exposure. When he finally got back to the bus we had been waiting for him for over an hour and he wasn't very popular with the other passengers.

A couple of hundred kilometres southwest of Kings Canyon can be found the iconic Uluru, the world's largest monolith. It isn't the largest rock, firstly, because it isn't a single rock, and secondly, that title belongs to Mount Augustus in Western Australia.

Even though it is a massive object sitting in a relatively flat landscape, as you drove towards it you didn't get your first glimpse until you were fairly close. The way the road approached Uluru, and the many sand dunes along the way tended to block your view. But Uluru is not the only monolith in the area. Apart from the well-known domes of nearby Kata Tjuta, there is also a large mesa called Mount Connor, the 3 monoliths lying in an almost straight line, with Uluru in the middle.

A favourite game staff liked to play with the passengers as we drove towards them was we would buy the first person to see The Rock a drink, but if they were wrong, they had to buy us a drink. Inevitably, someone would say they saw it and claim their prize. The only problem was, the first thing you see along the road is Mount Connor, and when you only get a quick glimpse it is easily mistaken for Uluru. I don't think I ever had to buy someone a drink.

Of course, once we got to Uluru we would let the passengers do the climb. I was meant to do it with them but unfortunately, my fear of heights wouldn't let me do anything more than get high enough to just touch the bottom of the chain, put there to help people up the steep climb. Even then, to get that high I had to sit down and inch my way up backwards until I touched it and then immediately make my way back down. Unofficially, this point is known as Chicken Rock. Since I couldn't do the climb, I had to bribe the driver or the cook to do it in my place, a deal that usually cost me extra chores or many drinks at the bar afterwards.

Although I have never climbed it, I have walked around the base many times and in a lot of ways that walk is a lot more interesting than the climb, or so I have been told. Since 2019 the climb has been closed and the chain removed, so any chance of me ever doing it has now been lost.

The only time I climbed anything out there was one of the domes at Kata Tjuta. At the time you were allowed to climb it and, unlike Uluru, the climb was a gentle slope up one side, so my acrophobia didn't get much beyond a manageable constant anxiety. Once at the top, the view was spectacular and well worth battling my fear.

Just 5 years later, it turns out I would be living at the Ayers Rock Resort and running my own business showing people the incredible night sky of Central Australia.

**Yulara**

In 1990 the Ayers Rock Resort advertised for someone to set up an observatory and conduct evening tours of the night sky for their patrons. Since I had been to the resort a dozen times before with my guiding job, I knew what to expect, so with the help of a few others, a close friend and I decided to apply.

Having a captive audience and crystal clear dark skies seemed the perfect opportunity to expand my love of the universe. It turns out I was right about the audience but unfortunately not so much about the clear sky. In 1990 the internet didn't exist, so we had to rely on information about yearly weather patterns provided by the resort and the Bureau of Meteorology. Unfortunately, once out there, we discovered that their definition and our definition of clear skies weren't quite the same, but we will come back to that.

For our contract submission, we photographed our equipment one sunny weekend from the top of Observatory Hill in Sydney, as we figured it would look better to have the city and harbour in the background rather than a blank wall. The photos turned out wonderfully, but shortly after we took the last picture, we noticed there were thunderstorms in the distance surrounding the city. So, before packing up the equipment, we indulged ourselves in a little bit of storm watching. This turned out to be a significant learning moment for all of us.

There were 3 storms: one to the north, one to the west and one to the south. As an understatement, the thunder and lightning from each were spectacular, and we lost track of time admiring the show. However, the next thing we knew, all 3 storms were rapidly converging onto the city.

Broken from the spell of the lightning display, we madly started to pack up the equipment but had unfortunately left it a fraction too late. We managed to get the smaller pieces inside in time, but at the very last moment, before armageddon struck in the form of a perfect storm, all we could do was desperately throw large plastic bags over the telescopes. The heavens then opened up in one of the most violent storms I've ever seen. We couldn't leave the gear out in the rain so, while they were still under the plastic bags, we pulled the telescopes apart and carefully transported them bit by bit to safety undercover, where we could then pack them away properly. Fortunately, none of the equipment was damaged, but I can't say the same about us. I will never forget standing in the wild storm, completely soaked, pulling the telescopes apart.

Anyway, we eventually submitted our proposal, and it was good enough to get us an interview and trial presentation. The resort would pay our travel and equipment transportation expenses, and we would get to show them what we could do. Initially, 3 of us went out: me, my business partner and our technical expert. I call him our technical expert, but he was, in fact, a friend who was just more technically inclined than we were. Once out there, we had a day to set up and conduct an evening for about a dozen of the resort's management.

The following day we were to fly home, but in the morning we did something that probably swayed their decision in our favour. The resort had paid for our equipment to be shipped out and, of course, was going to pay for it to be shipped back to Sydney. From our perspective though, we thought if they chose us we could avoid having our delicate gear making a 6,000 kilometre round trip by road if we left the equipment at the resort until they made their decision. If they chose us, we already had our equipment on-site, and if we weren't successful, all we had done was delay slightly what the resort was going to do anyway. We were thinking purely about moving around a lot of equipment, but in hindsight, I think it may have been the thing that influenced their decision towards us.

As you may have guessed, we did get the job, and that meant finishing up in Sydney and getting ready to move 2,000 kilometres away. I say 2,000 kilometres, but that's in a straight line. By road, it was more like 3,500 kilometres and a long way to drive with a van full of possessions. It took 3 days to get there but we made it with 2 days to spare before we were contracted to start operating.

Since this was a brand new venture for the resort, when we arrived there was no specific custom-made site for an observatory. That would come about 6 months later. In the interim, the plan was to use the existing amphitheatre as our 'observatory'. This was not ideal, as a large shade sail and trees blocked a lot of our view, but until something more suitable could be constructed, it served our needs well enough. Unfortunately, there was nowhere in the amphitheatre to store our gear, so, every night we had to carry the equipment from a motel room, across the road, down the stairs of the amphitheatre, onto the stage and set it up. At the end of the night, around midnight, we repeated the process in reverse. We were more than a little tired, but at least we were becoming fitter.

After a couple of months of this arduous regime, the resort built a temporary, closed-in area at the back of the amphitheatre stage so we could leave the equipment there. This saved a lot of effort but also brought with it a nasty surprise. Anyone who has been to the Australian Outback knows it is a truly spectacular place that is also home to some troublesome creatures. Within days of storing our equipment at the back of the stage, we found each evening that our gear would be covered in Redback spiders. They are not the most dangerous spider in the world, but they are still nasty.

After arriving at the resort and before our first official session, we figured we had better do a run through and familiarise ourselves with the Central Australian sky. Back in Sydney, it was easy to locate the main constellations, as you could only see the brighter stars and since only a limited number were visible, identifying the constellations was relatively easy. But when we looked up that first night in the Centre, there were so many stars visible, from horizon to horizon, that it was difficult even to locate the Southern Cross, one of the brightest and most recognisable constellations of all. This caused us a bit of concern. If we struggled with the Southern Cross, how could we conduct an hour and a half tour only one day from then?

We spent the next few hours working out how to locate and identify just 4 constellations, which we figured was sufficient to tell stories around and point out objects within their boundaries. The plan was to start simple and expand as time progressed. As these 4 slowly disappeared, we would add newly found constellations and objects to the repertoire. By the time a year had gone by, we were able to point out maybe 70 of the 88 constellations up there. The only ones missing were those too close to the North Celestial Pole for us to see.

Living at the resort was great and we soon settled into a daily routine, but getting a new business up and running meant we were working most of the time and certainly every day. People on the east coast would call us at 7 am (our time) asking for information and decisions while at the end of the day we wouldn't finish work until around midnight. Working every day and every night like this would eventually take its toll. After about 3 months one of us would crack and either have to go for a few days break to the town of Alice Springs (about 450 kilometres away) or fly back to Sydney for a week. That meant the other person had to do double time while the other was away. Because of this, once one of us returned, the other then usually needed a few days off. After another 3 months, the cycle would repeat itself.

Even so, we were able to make friends. Initially, because people would have to come to us for work-related astronomical experiences, but soon it was because people just wanted to get to know us. Of course, it helped that we had the sole contract to run all astronomical content in the resort and astronomy is something that most people were interested in. Even though we didn't have a lot of free time, we managed to go on social occasions whenever we could. Usually, these were daytime activities, as our nights were full, unless the weather intervened and we had to finish early.

A couple of the more interesting friend moments involved a pilot and a policeman.

If you ever take a joy flight around Uluru, do it in the morning. As the day progresses and the sand dunes heat up, they generate a lot of uneven thermals in the air, and that makes the flight quite bumpy. Consequently, flights tend to start happening just as the Sun begins to rise.

We were doing some preparation work one particular morning when a pilot friend knocked on the door. He had just returned from a flight and was looking extremely pale and shaken. It turns out that during his second flight of the morning he had run out of fuel and had to make a forced landing in the dunes. Thankfully, no one was injured, but I guess everyone was a bit shaken up over the incident, including my friend. Later on, we found out that, because of the quick turnaround between flights, the pilot would go in and greet the next lot of passengers while the ground crew would check and refuel the aircraft. The pilot would then do a quick check of the plane but essentially trust that the crew had done their job properly. On this occasion, they had refuelled the plane but neglected to put the fuel cap back on, so as the plane flew, fuel leaked out until the tank was empty and hence the required emergency landing. It took a few days but eventually, my friend started flying again.

Everybody knew everyone else in the town that serviced the resort. That meant friendships were often made with people that normally you would never have expected to make. That was the case with us when we became friends with one of the local policemen. One day he rang and said he was doing a drive around the region and would we like to come. Not wanting to miss an opportunity to get out of the resort for a few hours we agreed, not even bothering to find out where we were going. As it turns out, we headed towards the large salt lake to the north of the resort, Lake Amadeus.

Generally, people aren't allowed to go there, as it lies within aboriginal land, but the police are permitted as they have to do general checks to make sure things are alright. The trip out was rough, as the track wasn't used very often, and that made the cramped space in the 4WD even more uncomfortable. When we finally arrived at the lake we were glad to get out of the car.

Since the whole area rarely saw people or vehicles, the wildlife was abundant. There were herds of wild horses and camels in their hundreds. Kangaroos were everywhere. The lake itself was huge and pristine. The only sign that anything had been on it in the foreseeable past were animal prints. The isolation was palpable and you got the feeling that if something were to happen it would be years before anyone found your body. It was a long day and once we were back we had to go straight into our nightly activities, but it was one of the best days I've ever had.

Eventually, our contract ran out at the resort and it was time to move back to Sydney. The trip was almost uneventful, except for a premonition by my business partner.

A couple of nights before I had to drive my van back, he had a dream. He dreamt that when I got to the Erldunda Roadhouse, at the intersection of the Lassiter and Stuart Highways (drive 200 kilometres due east from Uluru and at the end of the road turn right), I would have an accident. Consequently, he decided to fly back and leave me to drive the 3,500 kilometres in 3 days by myself. As expected, I didn't have an accident at the intersection, but my friend still maintains that's why he didn't want to do the drive. On a recent trip I couldn't resist stopping ast the intersection and sending a picture to him to say I had made it through okay yet again.

The drive itself was uneventful except that it was long. The first night I stopped at a roadhouse, the only one for about 300 kilometres, but they were full. Since I was too tired to continue, I decided to stay in the roadhouse car park and sleep in the front seat of the van, the back being full of gear. Unfortunately, it was uncomfortable and I didn't sleep well. That meant I was awake early, and with nothing else to do at the roadhouse, I left.

Some advice about driving around the outback, put a little more thought into it than I did at that moment. I left before the petrol station opened, but I figured I had enough fuel to get to the next town, Woomera. I arrived there at 8 am, but its petrol station didn't open till about 10 am. Keen to keep going, for some unknown reason, I decided to push on towards Adelaide rather than wait the 2 hours. For the last 100 kilometres, the gauge on my petrol tank was below the empty line, and all I could think about was what would I do if I ran out of fuel. Would I leave the valuable telescopes and gear alone for hours while I hitched a lift to get some petrol? Would I stay with the car and hope someone would stop who had some to spare? I made it that time, but I have never let my tank run that low again.

I recently went back to Yulara for a holiday. It has changed a lot since I lived out there. The shopping precinct is larger, there are more accommodation options, and generally everything has been updated, including introducing more than the one colour (we called it Yulara Pink) for the buildings. My old accommodation is still there, although it is now public accommodation. Sadly, my old observatory decking has been dismantled and the area revegetated.

**New South Wales**

Back in Sydney, the first thing I noticed was how light-polluted the sky was. Growing up I never thought about it, but now that I had spent years under a gloriously dark night sky, I realised all I had in the city was just a handful of stars visible.

In the years since returning from The Centre, I've been lucky to do a bit more travelling and exploring, although, nowhere near as extensive as I had before.

Over the years, I've been fortunate to have had friends working at the Parkes Radiotelescope and the Australian Astronomical Observatory (that operates the large telescopes just outside the town of Coonabarabran in New South Wales) and because of them, I've been able to have private tours of the facilities.

On the drive to visit my mother living near the Queensland border, I would always pass signs pointing out the cave and hiding place of Thunderbolt, the infamous New England bushranger. I remember my grandmother, who came from the area, once telling us about how her parents (my great grandparents) were once visited on their farm by the bushranger, so on one return trip, I thought I'd stop and have a look. After a steep climb down a rough track through the bush, I came to the cave that was supposedly Thunderbolt's hideout, and I have to say I was extremely underwhelmed. It was small, difficult to get to, and not the place I would want to hide in for more than one desperate night. Given the location in the sandstone and granite mountains of the New England range, I would have thought he could find a much better cave. Plus, he might be able to hide himself from any pursuing police, but his horse would have had to stay outside, not exactly invisible to people searching for him.

**Tasmania**

In my tour guiding days I visited every state in the country except Tasmania. In 2010 and then again in 2019, I was able to rectify this when a group of friends and I toured around the island state, both times in the first half of January. We picked that timing as it was the only period we could all get off work and, as it turns out, it was the best time to visit the island. Even in January, places were cold, getting down to single digits during the night, but other friends have visited in early December and encountered snow on Cradle Mountain, located in the centre of the island. Despite the cold, Tasmania is a beautiful place to visit.

On the first trip, we went across on the boat from Melbourne overnight, staying in sleeping cabins. Bass Strait is shallow and as such, notoriously often quite rough. On the trip over the boat would rise up as it went over a wave and then crash down, only to repeat the process as it went over the next wave. This made lying in bed quite entertaining and relaxing, at least for me. Some of my friends didn't find it quite so enjoyable and didn't get much sleep.

The second time we flew down, rather than catch the boat, and unfortunately, it was the second trip that I spent the whole time limping around the island with a badly torn Achilles Tendon.

Volcano caldera on the Big Island of Hawai'i

Waikiki Beach on the island of O'ahu

Fisherman's Wharf in San Francisco, California

The Grand Canyon

A grove of redwood trees in Sequoia-Kings Canyon National Parks

The 'General Sherman' tree, the largest living thing on the planet (based on volume)

Yosemite Valley

Meteor (Barringer) Crater

Camping and canoeing weekend away, northwest of Sydney

Camping and bike riding weekend away, north of Sydney

Driving down a track in the Warrumbungle National Park, NSW

Barron Falls, west of Cairns, FNQ

Port Douglas beach from a nearby lookout

Crossing the Wenlock River, Cape York

An anthill on Cape York

The most northerly point on the Australian mainland

Creek crossing near Bamaga, Cape York

Beach at the tip of Cape York

The Gulf of Carpentaria at Karumba, QLD

Mount Isa, QLD

Queensland - Northern Territory border on the Barkley Tablelands

The town of Tibooburra, NSW

Monument to the explorers Burke and Wills at Cooper Creek, Innamincka QLD

Sign at the intersection of the Stuart Highway and Oodnadatta Track, South Australia

Hotel at William Creek, halfway along the Ooodnadatta Track

Lake Eyre South from a distance

Woomera, South Australia

Coober Pedy, South Australia

The Breakaways, South Australia

A Boab tree in the Kimberley region, Western Australia

Kununurra, Kimberley region, Western Australia

The Western Australia - Northern Territory boundary down the Tanami Track

The Bungle Bungles, Kimberley Region, Western Australia

Wolfe Creek Crater, down the Tanami Track from Halls Creek, Western Australia

Henbury Meteorite Crater, Northern Territory

Me, somewhere down the Tanami Track

Cable Beach, Broome, Western Australia

Iron ore being loaded onto a tanker, Port Hedland, Western Australia

Whale shark off Ningaloo Reef, Exmouth, Western Australia

Exmouth, Western Australia

Kalbarri Skywalk, Kalbarri National Park, Western Australia

Grove of Karri trees, Western Australia

Valley of the Giants Treetop Walk, Western Australia

Wave Rock, Western Australia

Hippos Mouth, Wave Rock National Park, Western Australia

90 Mile Straight, Nullabor, Western Australia

Storms over the Nullabor at Eucla, Western Australia

The Bunda Cliffs, Nullabor, South Australia

Katherine Gorge, Northern Territory

Katherine Gorge, Northern Territory

The Devils Marbles, Northern Territory

A single Devils Marble

Daly Waters Pub, Northern Territory

The Plenty Highway at Glenormiston, just inside the Queensland border

Sand dunes on the edge of the Simpson Desert

The start of the Birdsville Track at Marree, South Australia

The start of the Birdsville Track

The town of Birdsville, southwest Queensland

Alice Springs, Northern Territory

The Finke River, the oldest riverbed in the world

The Alice Springs camel farm

Kings Canyon, Northern Territory

Kings Creek at the bottom of Kings Canyon

Pool of water and associated snake at the end of Kings Creek

Mount Connor, Northern Territory

Uluru from a distance, Northern Territory

The base of the Uluru climb showing Chicken Rock (where people are grouped)

Moonrise over Uluru

Uluru

Kata Tjuta from a distance

Close up of some Kata Tjuta domes

Walking around Kata Tjuta

Moonrise over Kata Tjuta

Our temporary observatory set up in the resort's amphitheatre

Early morning flight over Uluru

Camels on the way to Lake Amadeus

Lake Amadeus

Radiotelescope dishes just outside Narrabri, New South Wales

Siding Spring Observatory, Warrumbungle National Park, New South Wales

The Anglo-Australian Telescope at Siding Spring Observatory

Thunderbolt's Cave

Hobart harbour, Tasmania

The Gordon River in southwestern Tasmania

The oldest stone span bridge in Australia, located in the town of Richmond, Tasmania

The rugged northwest corner of Tasmania

Cradle Mountain in the centre of Tasmania

Port Arthur ruins in southeastern Tasmania

CHAPTER 8

# The Natural World

—

Like all Australians, I have a love-hate relationship with the local inhabitants. In particular, the creepy-crawly ones. Yet it is impossible not to interact with them at some point.

**Spiders and Snakes**

Growing up in Sydney with the deadliest spider in the world, the Sydney Funnel Web, meant the other spider varieties found in the region didn't bother me all that much, they were just an annoyance. Even the Funnel Web Spiders were really just an inconvenience when you grew up with them.

My grandmother's back yard was riddled with Funnel Web holes, and whenever we visited, we knew there were safe areas and paths to follow. Venture outside these areas, and you had to be wary, very wary, but it was never a case of not doing so if needed.

The house my grandmother lived in was old and at one point needed to have the electrical wiring replaced throughout the entire building. My uncle was an electrician, so offered to do the work in order to save money. However, the confusing thing to me was that he had 4 sons, yet when the time came to do the work, I was the one who had to help him.

The work was tedious until he said I had to crawl under the house to tack up all the wiring, instead of letting it dangle down. Then it became scary. Since the space under the house was not very high, I couldn't crawl, so it meant I had to lie on my back and shuffle around, hammering the clamps onto the wooden bearers and hooking the wire into them. The problem was that I was acutely aware of the volume of Funnel Web spiders that might exist under there and I was potentially going to be sharing the confined space with them. I voiced my concerns, and the solution my uncle came up with, rather than not doing it, was to use 2 sheets of cardboard. I would lie on one, move the other ahead of me and then shuffle onto it. By repeating the process, I could make my way around and hopefully, the cardboard would block any holes and protect me from the spiders. I did mention that even if it worked in the moment, I would just be creating an army of angry spiders that would come after me when I moved on, but it seemed to fall on deaf ears and I had to do it anyway. It was the longest 30 minutes I think I've ever spent, as every second I expected to see a deadly spider right beside my face, arched back and ready to strike.

Years after my grandmother died, I drove past her house and noticed it had been demolished and a new house built on the site. I bet the workmen that built the house got a huge surprise when they dug up all those angry Funnel Web spiders!

Living near the edge of the bush on the outskirts of Sydney, we also occasionally found aggressive Funnel Webs inside the house, but again, that was just part of growing up.

Not all spiders are dangerous. At our house in Berowra, we had a lot of Orb Weaver spiders that built their webs across our driveway and front yard. How they built the web across the yard was always a mystery, as it was easily 15 metres of open space between the trees. But every day we would break the webs down and every morning we found these enormous webs had been rebuilt. It got so bad that we used to keep a stick near the front door and another at the top of the driveway so we had something to wave in front of us as we walked to the car. If you forgot to use the stick you very quickly ended up with a face full of web, or worse, spider.

Like every house in Australia, there were also plenty of Huntsman spiders inside. These look fearsome, as they can be quite large, but are really quite harmless. In a lot of ways, they are also beneficial to have, as they help control the insect population. Unfortunately, very few people will tolerate having any spider in the house and either kill or relocate them.

When we first moved into the house I shared a room with one of my brothers. We had bunk beds and I was on the top. One evening, there was a Huntsman on the ceiling, directly above my bed and, still being very young, asked my brother to move it. Instead of getting rid of the spider, he picked up a shoe and squashed it against the ceiling and for the next 10 years, I had to look at the stain from the squashed spider every night as I lay in bed. It wasn't until my father repainted the house that I was able to get rid of it.

That wasn't my only run-in with a Huntsman.

I was in the car with my sister and mother one day as we drove down the highway when suddenly mum swerved off the road and slammed on the brakes. She jumped out of the car, along with my sister, all without letting me know why. Once they were out, I saw that on the inside roof of the car there was a giant Huntsman. After I had also exited the car, mum told me, without any hint that it might be open for debate, to get rid of it. Not knowing how to do that, I did the only thing I could think of, I grabbed it with my hand and quickly threw it out of the car. That was the first time I had a spider in my hands, but not the last.

By the time I was in university I had moved into the room we had built under the house, as it provided a bit more independence and privacy. The problem was that it wasn't as secure from spider invasion as the main house was. One night I was lying in bed, reading a book, when something suddenly plopped onto the pillow beside my head, a large Huntsman spider. I've never got out of bed so quickly before or since.

On another evening I was drifting off to sleep when I felt a tickling on my right leg. Thinking it was just an itch, I rubbed my leg with my hand before removing it from under the sheets. As I did so, I thought that it hadn't felt quite right, it felt like something soft had rolled between my hand and my leg. I quickly put my hand back, grabbed the offending soft object and pulled it out, only to see it was a Huntsman spider that had been crawling up my leg. I immediately leapt out of bed and before I even contemplated getting back in, stripped the bed completely, vigorously shook all the sheets and did a thorough search of the room to see if there were any more lurking around, just waiting for their chance to crawl under my sheets.

We also had Redback spiders around the house, but these weren't quite as common. That situation changed when I moved out to Uluru in Central Australia and found that they were everywhere.

As mentioned in the last chapter, when we first set up our observatory in the Ayers Rock Resort amphitheatre and a storage room was built for us at the back of the stage area, we found that within days our gear would be covered in Redback spiders each evening. Not the most dangerous spider in the world, but it's still a good policy to avoid being bitten by one. The solution was not to panic, or use copious amounts of spray, but to leave a rock near the door. Each night we would pick up the rock, open the door and before we touched any piece of equipment, squash any spiders that happened to be on it. The method worked well.

Since we very quickly became unworried by the spiders, when my mother visited and found a large Redback in my apartment and started to stress out, I simply squashed it and continued on with our conversation. I don't think mum was quite as calm about the whole incident.

While working out of the amphitheatre, things would occasionally take an exciting turn when we found a snake amongst our equipment, but we survived those moments as well. These weren't harmless either. They were Western Brown snakes, among the deadliest in the world, so some caution had to be encouraged. Once we moved into our permanent location and had a purpose-built shed to store our equipment, spiders and snakes became less of an issue.

I don't like snakes and I think more than any other creature they scare me the most. It doesn't help that we have so many dangerous ones. Any snake you come across is too big and too fast to simply step on (like a spider), or avoid being in their domain (like a crocodile or shark), and more than likely they will be venomous. Yet, for some reason, I seem to have run across more than my fair share.

Apart from the occasional Brown Snake at the Ayers Rock resort, we used to have Death Adders travel across our back yard in Sydney. Mum would often be hanging out the washing and suddenly state the simple fact "snake", which meant get off the lawn and wait for it to move past and disappear back into the bush.

At my brother's farm, snakes were just a part of life, often eating the eggs in the barn, being cut into pieces as we chainsawed a log into firewood, or simply falling out of ceiling exhaust fans into the bath.

I was walking along the driveway with my niece one day, she was slightly in front, when she abruptly turned, sprinted the 20 metres to the nearest fence and leapt onto the top of a wooden fence post. Then she started to point and that's when I noticed a snake was crossing the driveway about 10 metres in front of me. We waited for it to move on before progressing.

When I lived at my friend's farm for a year, Brown Snakes were also an issue. I would walk out of the front door of a morning to find a 2 metre long snake sunning itself on the driveway beside the car, before quickly slithering off when it saw me. When I put bird netting over my vegetable patch to stop the birds from eating the fruit, the netting would inevitably catch a snake as it became tangled in the netting on the ground. This would always catch me by surprise as I was mowing the lawn. Concentrating on the mowing I would get to the patch and turn the corner of the bed to suddenly see a wriggling snake right in front of me. I would have to dispatch it first and then cut it out of the netting before continuing.

But the snake encounter that scared me the most was when my mother moved from her farm into a house in town. At the farm, she had cultivated some impressive flower beds, in particular, a remarkable variety of orchids. The whole family was there to help her pack and move and of course, we couldn't leave the orchids without taking some to transplant in town and at each of our homes. We dug the plants up and put them into individual plastic garbage bags, one for each of us and one for mum. We didn't leave straight away so they were sitting in the yard for about half an hour.

When we did leave, we each put a bag in our car and left. I was going back to the house with mum and when we got there, I figured I should plant the orchids straight away, so I tore open the bag and started to pull the plants apart in order to spread them out a bit. It was at that point that a baby brown snake reared its head and was looking very, very agitated. As it was right beside my hand and I was bending over, so my face was also quite close, I was extremely nervous. Even baby snakes are deadly, so it was a tense situation. Fortunately, it took off in the direction opposite to where I was standing, but I was still badly shaken. Since it must have been in the bag from out at the farm and since where there is one baby snake, chances are there will be more, I quickly called the others to be careful and check their bags. It seemed luck was on our side and the bag I opened was the only one that had a snake hitching a ride with us.

**Insects**

While snakes and spiders are a concern, insects are just annoying.

My eldest brother moved out of the house when I was still in my early teens, enabling me to finally have a room of my own.

I don't remember it happening when I shared a room with my other brother, but almost as soon as I moved into the new room I had a mosquito problem. The mosquitoes didn't bother me, either through acquired immunity or the teenage ability to sleep through anything, but every morning I would wake up to find the ceiling black with the pesky little insects. If you think this is an exaggeration, you would be wrong. Each morning I would get out of bed very slowly, careful not to disturb them, and use half a can of insect spray before closing the door. Given the amount of spray required, I would have to give it 30 minutes before I could venture back in, and when I did, there would be dead mosquitoes over everything. I would have to wipe them off the desk, off the cupboard, and strip the bed and give the sheets a good shake. Once that was done, I had to vacuum the carpet to clear their dead bodies. This happened EVERY day.

Where they came from, we never found out. Mosquitoes need still water to breed and there certainly wasn't any of that in my room, or around the house and yard generally. I could have closed the window to try and keep them out, but I needed to have it open to get some air circulation, especially in summer. There was a fly screen over the window, but it seemed to be completely ineffective at stopping mosquitoes. The problem was only resolved once I moved out.

I still don't know why it occurred, but for whatever reason it did, I seem to have built up an immunity to them. Even now, I can be outside with friends and they will whine and complain about a single mosquito, insisting we go indoors to escape it when I hadn't noticed a thing.

Like everything else in the outback, even the insects are supersized.

Working at the Ayers Rock Resort we discovered that there were distinct seasons for the flying pests, and when they happened, they were either the largest individuals I have ever seen or the largest swarm I've ever encountered. When you are trying to show a group of tourists through a telescope, it is difficult to do so when you are being attacked by monsters.

Flies were a daytime constant but thankfully disappeared when the Sun went down. However, once the Sun set, we were then beset by other problems.

The first one we encountered were Stick Insects, thousands each night flying around us, with some individuals easily measuring 30 centimetres long. At one point we contemplated buying a tennis racket so we could swat them away while people tried to look through the telescopes. Every night for about a month they would appear and then suddenly, they disappeared, only to be replaced by a mammoth swarm of moths every night. The moths plagued us for about another month before they too abruptly disappeared, only to have them immediately replaced by flying beetles. The beetles ranged in size from quite small to large enough to give you a concussion if they flew into your head at speed. Thankfully, they only hung around for about a month as well.

Apart from these swarms over the summer months, insects weren't a problem after sunset in winter. However, during the day all year round, flies were something you could not avoid.

Winter months, they were manageable. Summer months, you either got used to swallowing multiple flies every time you breathed or opened your mouth to speak, or you wore a net over your head. The net may have looked silly, but it worked.

In summer the number of flies in your immediate vicinity could be counted in the billions, and that always raised a question in my head. No matter where you are, you are surrounded by countless flies. Get in a car and drive 50 kilometres down the road and as soon as you stop and get out you are once again immediately surrounded by innumerable flies. Since you were driving faster than any fly can travel, that means the flies were there when you arrived. So, if there are that many flies everywhere in the countryside, why when you look into the distance doesn't the view look more and more distorted the further away you look? With so many of them, would you not be looking through an ever-thickening cloud of flies, creating a grey haze you have to peer through? I have yet to resolve this conundrum to my satisfaction.

## Cats and Dogs

As a family, we never had a dog as a pet, only cats.

The first cat I can remember belonged to my grandmother. I have no idea of its breed since to a young me it was just a cat, but I do remember it was black all over and big. Plus, it was vicious to everyone, including my grandmother, except me. Apparently, I was the only one it would allow to pet him.

But the cat I loved the most was our family pet for many years. It had the most beautiful nature and was remarkably well trained, at least as much as cats can be trained. It would frequently sleep at my feet under the sheets of my bed, so of an evening she would head down the hallway and into my bedroom in anticipation for when I went to bed. My father wasn't keen on her doing that, so if he saw her heading down the hallway he would simply say "No", and without missing a step, she would turn around and walk back into the living room as if she always meant to do exactly that. Of course, she would try again the next night as my father didn't always see her.

Being an affectionate cat, she would also want to sit in your lap, purring so loudly we would often have to turn the volume up on the television. As she got older, she would also start to dribble as she purred and her need to always be close to one us would manifest itself in strange ways.

Every Sunday we would pick up our grandmother and bring her home to have lunch with us. As my grandmother got older, she required walking sticks to get around, and when it came to climbing the front steps of our house it was a process that required our help. Because it was a slow climb with a few of us assisting, our cat felt she should also be part of the action. She would jump onto the railing and walk down it until she met my grandmother coming up the steps. Once there, all the while purring and dribbling, she would then climb onto my grandmother's shoulders and lie across them until we had all made it inside the house. I know our cat enjoyed doing it and I suspect my grandmother was just as pleased.

After I moved into a house with a number of friends, we didn't have any pets to begin with, unless you count the mice we had in the house due to a mouse plague.

We had become used to having mice run across the floor and catching 3 or 4 a night in traps, that we no longer gave the sight of another mouse scuttling around a second thought. One afternoon a friend called in and, while we were sitting in the lounge room, a mouse made an appearance. We ignored it but the friend was horrified. He stood up, said "I'll be back soon", and left. About 20 minutes later he arrived back bearing a gift, one of the kittens his cat had recently given birth to. Over the next few weeks, the kitten did its job and got rid of our mouse issue, but the problem was, as it grew older it seemed to want to be around us and always be wherever we were, but absolutely refused to be picked up or petted.

After finishing work one night I arrived home about 11:45 pm. I always find it hard to go straight to bed after work, so I sat up for a bit watching television. About midnight I heard a car come down the street and then a few minutes later, a knock on the door. It was our next-door neighbour letting me know that our cat was, unfortunately, lying in the middle of the road, dead. I hadn't seen it when I drove down only 15 minutes earlier and the only car I had heard since arriving home was theirs, so it occurred to me that it must have been me that ran over our cat. At 12:30 am, myself and my neighbour went out, picked up the cat from the road and buried it in the backyard. The following morning, I came out of my room to find our neighbour's 2 young daughters in the backyard, crying and placing flowers on the cat's grave.

From then on, we only had dogs in the house.

Dogs and I have a mutual understanding. We don't like each other unless I've known them since they were young puppies.

I could be in a crowd of people and if a stray dog comes up to the group it will walk past everyone else and immediately find me. This happened one night when we parked on a street outside a car yard. The owner of the yard was there and didn't like us parking out front, so they let their guard dog out of the gate. Immediately it ran past all my friends and stood snarling, teeth bared, mere centimetres from my leg. The owner was threatening us with the dog when all they had to do was ask us to move and we would have been happy to do so.

Another time I was crossing the road to get to the local post office and a mother with her 2 young children and a small dog was walking along the footpath. I deliberately walked a bit wider than I had to in order to avoid the dog, but as I passed them the dog ran across the intervening 3 metres and bit me on the heel. It was only small, so it didn't hurt, but I wasn't in the mood for an animal to bite me for no reason, so my first thought was that it wasn't very big and I could probably kick it to the far side of the road quite easily. I was about to do so when I realised the kids were crying and the mother was apologising non-stop, so I paused, thinking it would certainly make me feel better, but upset the kids even more. Consequently, I let it live that day and continued on my way.

On a more positive side, in the house, a friend came home one day with a dog but didn't tell me beforehand. They all knew how I would react so left it for me to find out when I got home from work. The problem was, it was a Rottweiler. Fortunately, it was a puppy and he grew up to be a great dog and a fabulous guard dog. If you were a stranger and came in the front door he would be all over you wanting non-stop pats and slobbering profusely. Jump the side gate, however, and you would regret doing so.

Other friends have had dogs that I like, but once again, that's because we knew each other from the time they were puppies. The only exception to that rule was a dog my mother bought when she lived out on her farm, a blue cattle dog. He was the best friend anyone could have had. If you were family, he loved you. If you were a stranger, he was never going to let you near his family without permission. He was also an expert at catching and killing snakes.

Unfortunately, when mum moved into the house in town, he became the unwanted focus of a local man who agisted some horses in a vacant paddock next to my mother's place. Even though he never went near the horses, the person claimed he was harassing them and mum had to get rid of him, something she was never going to do, as he was a great companion for her. I was visiting one day and went for a walk with the dog through the paddock. There were no horses around, so I didn't think anything about it and let him wander a bit, but always within sight. Once back from the walk we got in the car and headed out to my brother's farm for lunch. About 3 minutes into the trip, the dog started getting agitated and jumped from the back seat to under my feet as I was driving. He started running around the front seat area and defecating everywhere. Scared, we quickly drove him to the vet where he stayed overnight, but the following morning we received the news that he had died. He had been poisoned. My mother, along with myself, were devastated.

It turns out that dog baits had been laid in the vacant paddock, apparently specifically to target my mother's dog. It is illegal to place baits in residential areas. Even on rural properties, state forests and national parks, you must inform any neighbours so they can take appropriate precautions with their animals. Mum didn't have any more pets after that incident.

**Cattle**

Cats and dogs are not the only animals I've had contact with. Working with my friend on his farm meant dealing with cattle up close and personal. Anything from tagging and drenching to de-balling steers, to pulling calves from cows, and shooting sick animals was on the table. Given we were both city boys, it was all a case of learning what to do as we went along. One thing we didn't count on was the individual personalities the animals had, especially in the steers. It seemed that in every generation there was at least one crazy animal, and once identified, they tended to be the first ones on the truck for the sale yards.

On one occasion my friend got a call from his neighbour, saying that a steer had jumped the fence and was in amongst his cows. We figured it would simply be a case of going over, herding him out the gate, down the road and back into the friend's property. Unfortunately, it wasn't that simple.

I drove the farm ute over while my friend took the quad bike. As he went up the paddock to start driving the steer towards the gate I hung back, blocking off a possible escape route. I wasn't paying much attention, only glancing occasionally to see if he was getting closer and I would have to start doing something. I could see he was having trouble getting the steer to head in the right direction but didn't think too much about it. When I glanced up after about 10 minutes, I saw that my friend was off the bike and being chased around it by the mad steer. They were 200 metres away so it took a minute to get over there but I raced as fast as I could to get between the steer and my friend, hopefully before he got trampled to death.

The idea was, get between the 2 of them with the car so my friend had a chance to get on the bike and out of the way. The plan worked and I managed to separate them, but now I had a crazy animal staring me down. I figured I would be best having the front of the car, with the bull bar, facing directly at the steer, and I was right. After staring at each other for a few seconds, the steer charged and head-butted the bull bar. It rocked the car but also stunned the steer. Figuring now was the time to retreat and deal with the animal later, after it had calmed down, we left, telling the neighbour we would be back.

I wasn't there when my friend tried again a few days later, but instead of running it back to his property my friend simply ran it through the neighbour's yards and straight onto the truck taking it to the sale yards.

**Prawns and Toads**

Some other animal interactions weren't quite so adrenaline-filled, but still interesting in their own way. I've been prawn fishing in a lake near Port Macquarie where we had to wade out into the lake, dragging a net between us, before hauling it back onto the beach to collect our catch.

At a caravan park just south of Cairns, if you got up in the middle of the night to go to the amenities block you couldn't lift your feet off the ground as you walked, you had to slide them. If you picked your foot up it was impossible to put it back down without stepping on a cane toad, they were so thick on the ground. And standing in the toilet block you were surrounded by dozens of sets of eyes as the toads were all over the walls and floor.

## Birds

I never realised how lucky I was surrounded by bush living on the outskirts of Sydney in terms of the birdlife we encountered. Galahs, magpies, rosellas and sulphur-crested cockatoos were everywhere. Occasionally a flock of the rarer black cockatoos would perch in a tree beside the house. And most amazing of all, there were lyrebirds in the bush below us. We could hear them calling quite often and very occasionally one could be seen wandering just inside the edge of the bush beside the house. As the area became more and more built up, the lyrebirds unfortunately disappeared.

Many years later, at my mother's house up north, she would hand feed some king parrots. If you sat quietly they would land on the railing a metre from you and eat the seeds mum put out for them.

On a slightly larger scale, I've seen a lot of emus and cassowaries in the wild, but one day we were having lunch in a town called Emu Park, in Queensland, where they got too close for comfort and became a problem. I guess the town name should have been a giveaway, but while we were eating, dozens of the birds came down to steal food from us. If you have never seen an emu up close, they are big, strong birds, so having one lean over your shoulder and try and steal your sandwich can be quite intimidating. There was no way I could physically push them away, so the only option I could come up with to keep them at bay while everyone hurriedly finished their lunch, was to tap them with a wooden tent pole, constantly herding them away. I then ate lunch once we were on the move again.

## Kangaroos

If you ever drive on country roads for more than an hour, chances are you will have either hit a kangaroo or narrowly missed hitting one. Having to slam on the brakes as one bounds in front of you is always a possibility, especially if driving early morning or late afternoon. Sometimes they will run into you, hitting the side of the car with a thud, and sometimes the 2 of you will collide head-on. Depending on the size of the roo and the speed you are travelling will determine the extent of the damage you experience.

Over the years I have hit quite a few roos, some harder than others.

Some just rolled under the car or bounced off before bounding away. The first one I hit smashed the front of the car so badly it was undrivable. We were on holiday at the time and we managed to get the car running enough to get us home, but we were picking kangaroo fur and chunks of meat out of the grill for weeks.

Living in The Centre meant a whole new level of potential kangaroo collisions. They are everywhere, and big.

Every night we were paid to meet a tour out at Kata Tjuta. The passengers would go for a walk in the afternoon and then have a bar-b-que dinner while watching the Sun set over the domes. While the driver was cleaning up and packing the gear away, we were then employed to entertain the passengers by giving a star talk. Because there was no need for me to be out there early, when the bus took them out, I would drive and meet them for dinner, give the star talk, then drive back to help my partner with the sessions at our observatory. A few times, when I was running late and perhaps driving a little too fast, I would come across kangaroos or camels in the middle of the road. Having to pull up in a van from 140 km/hr in the space of a few metres is more than enough to get your heart racing. Kangaroos are impressive enough, but a camel whose stomach is the same height as your windshield suddenly appearing in front of you is another level of awesome.

## Night Skies

Apart from the wildlife, one of the best things about the nighttime drive was that you were kilometres from *any* source of light. If there was complete cloud cover, so not even stars visible, the night would be pitch black. A few times as I was driving, I would turn off my car headlights to see what it was like and found I could not see a metre in front of the car. It was total blackness. Animals were not the only way to get your heart rate up on that drive.

If you have never been to a really dark place in the country, do yourself a favour and go. Faint stars are visible right down to the horizon and the Milky Way leaps out at you. There are so many stars it seems you couldn't count them all (although, theoretically the figure is only about 3,000 individual stars visible to the eye at any one time, but I think that bit of information spoils the spectacle). And faint objects viewed through the telescope stand there in all their glory.

During my time in Central Australia, I managed to see so many objects that I had only ever read about before. In particular, those visible with just binoculars and my eyes. While my partner was conducting his part of the evening tour and I was momentarily free, my favourite pastime was to lie on my back, off to the side, and stare at the incredible night sky. I know it isn't possible, but I swear I could see the Milky Way in 3 dimensions during these times.

I also came to appreciate just how much the Moon affects our view. From a town or city with light pollution, the effect the Moon's light has on your view isn't noticeable, as artificial lighting interferes just as much, if not more. But with no artificial lighting, the Moon's light is dramatic.

**Weather**

Another thing I came to appreciate was the weather. What I consider to be cloudy weather, and what the majority of people call cloudy weather is not necessarily the same. Most people thought it clear as long as it wasn't raining. This is not a great definition when trying to use a telescope.

But cloudy weather in Central Australia does have an upside, even for an astronomer. I have always loved thunderstorms, and the storms in the desert are spectacularly amazing with most consisting of a single cloud delivering a fantastic lightning display. If the storm passed over you, the rain was torrential but would stop quickly once the cloud moved on. Since the desert is mostly flat, this torrential downpour has nowhere to go, so the resort would temporarily flood until the water soaked into the ground. These were great opportunities to race outside with a cloth and wash my car. Water is precious out there, and you weren't allowed to wash your car any other time, so I couldn't let the opportunity pass.

The other thing with storms was you could always tell who was a local when it rained. They were the ones heading toward Uluru while it was raining to see water cascading off it. An incredible sight to behold when it happens. Tourists were the ones heading from Uluru to the resort because they didn't want to get wet.

Often storms would pass by off to the side. During these times, we had crystal clear skies overhead and the storm's fantastic display in the distance. Occasionally we would just have to stop and watch the storm for a few minutes before carrying on with our stargazing.

Of course, there were also times when it was completely cloudy, and desert weather is notorious for changing within minutes. On one night the weather was clear, no breeze, and balmy. People arrived for the evening tour and, because of the weather, we had a big crowd, around 50 people. I had finished taking the admission fees and mustered everyone together to introduce myself when I noticed a cloud front moving in quickly. Within 2 minutes, it had completely covered the entire sky. I hadn't even finished welcoming everyone before I had to call the night off and hand the money back. Thankfully it was dark so people couldn't see me crying as I did so.

Before I leave the weather in Central Australia, I have to mention sand storms. Frequent and massive in extent, if I saw one coming I had to rush around putting towels against the gaps under doors, around windows and make sure all telescope equipment was tightly packed up. Even so, the sand and dust got everywhere. If your clothes and shoes weren't red to begin with, they certainly were after a few sand storms.

Now, if you are a space buff, red sand, rocks and dust storms may sound familiar. Take away the spinifex and mulga bushes (plus a few other bits and pieces of flora and fauna) and you would find Central Australia and Mars look very similar, and for the same reason. The sand and rocks in both places have a small amount of iron oxide (also known as rust) in them, and that gives them their reddish appearance.

Incidentally, I love the desert, but here's a tip. If you ever visit spinifex country DO NOT touch the spiky grass, it is nasty. The spikes have needle-like tips that break off in the skin and cause their victim no end of grief for days.

Sand storms in the centre are not the only ones I have lived through. Every so often Sydney would be blanketed by a dust storm and after years of drought in the country, my adopted town of Orange in the Central West of NSW would have a dust storm pass over at least once a week for months on end.

But the best dust storm has to be the one we encountered on the afternoon of Day 3 during the Murray River Canoe Marathon.

The third day of the race was thankfully short, only about 76 kilometres, so we were able to finish mid-afternoon. Looking forward to having a longer than usual rest, we went back to the campsite to lie down for a few hours before having to worry about dinner. But, before we could get more than 30 minutes of peace, a huge dust storm was spotted heading our way.

Our camp consisted of smaller sleeping tents and because there was so many of us, one large, open, communal tent, borrowed from a friend in the army. As the front of the dust storm approached, we hastily checked and tightened all tent ropes and pegs and made sure everything was closed and, hopefully, dustproof. We weren't the only ones, as the entire campground was madly making preparations. The larger, communal tent was always going to be a problem. It was only ever meant to be a gathering place, providing a bit of shelter from any potential rain and so only had walls on 3 sides, and those weren't exactly sealed to keep out dust.

As the storm front arrived, the wind was incredibly strong, whipping the dust to the point where you could not see more than 10 metres and it stung any exposed flesh. The smaller tents were madly blown around but seemed to be holding okay. The same couldn't be said for other people's tents as a number of them could be seen cartwheeling across the ground. Our larger tent, however, was causing us a lot of issues. With a larger surface area exposed to the full force of wind and dust, it was acting like a huge sail. Although we had put on extra ropes and pegs, the force being exerted on it was threatening to rip them out of the ground and turn it into a deadly weapon by sending it flying across the campground.

To stop this, we realised we needed to anchor it down more firmly. Given the conditions, the only thing we could think of was to add our own weight. So, at one point there were 10 of us hanging onto different parts of the tent frame, trying to weigh it down and keep it from sailing away, all the while being sandblasted by the dust.

Eventually, the storm passed but it took a while to sort things out and clean our gear. So much for recuperating and enjoying a relaxing afternoon off from paddling.

Another storm that was even more destructive occurred while I was visiting my mother in northern NSW. It was the last day before I was heading home and we had organised an auto electrician in the town of Lismore to install a sound system we had recently bought for mum's car. We were meant to be there about 2 pm so, rather than heading straight to Lismore, we decided to have lunch in a town on the way. As we ate lunch, we could hear snippets of people's conversations about a wild storm in the area and as the sky darkened, we quickly finished and decided to get to the auto electrician as soon as possible. What we didn't know at the time was we were heading straight into the storm.

About halfway there we encountered the first bits of hail and very quickly it escalated to the point where the hail was about the size of the end of your thumb and being blown horizontally. It was so thick that you could not see any further than the front of the car. Since we were driving, this posed enormous risks, so I was desperate to find somewhere I could pull off the road and wait it out. Eventually, I found a spot and stopped the car, with the back window facing the direction of the hail. I expected it to be smashed at any moment but figured it would still provide some protection.

The punishment the car took that day from the hail was incredible. I fully expected the paint to be flayed from the car and to have every panel severely dented. But in a remarkable testament to how tough cars can be, despite the battering, there was not a single mark. When the storm finally subsided and we could see more than 2 metres we found that we were not the only cars stopped in the area. There were about a dozen vehicles and it was amazing that none of us had hit another car when we pulled off the road.

After continuing on to Lismore we discovered the devastation the storm had wreaked on the town. We had experienced just the edge of the storm, but Lismore had worn the full brunt of it. Hail the size of cricket balls were lying everywhere. Almost every window and shopfront in the town was smashed and cars were destroyed. Even the shopfronts that had an awning over them were smashed, as the large hailstones simply bounced off the roads and footpaths and crashed into the shop front glass. Despite the damage to the town, we continued to the auto electrician and although reluctant to do the job, given what had just happened, we talked him into it, as it was the only chance we would have before I went home.

I've already mentioned a few times that I love storms, although the Lismore episode made me realise I prefer to watch them and not necessarily participate.

In particular, I love thunderstorms that produce a lot of lightning, but once again, from a distance and not as an active lightning rod.

On a couple of occasions, like the Lismore hail storm, I haven't had the luxury of seeing lightning from afar and have come way too close to it for my liking.

Perhaps the most dangerous time was working in the middle of a paddock on my friend's farm. It was an overcast day, more like the type that produces drizzly rain than a thunderstorm, when out of nowhere a lightning strike occurred in the paddock we were currently working. Since it had appeared with no warning and we were the highest points for hundreds of metres around, it was terrifying. We had no idea if there was going to be a second strike and if there was, whether it would be centred on one of us. Needless to say, we finished work for the day and went inside.

The second time was a lot more spectacular. Still dangerous, but less so because I was in a car at the time.

Having just dropped off my grandmother from her regular Sunday lunch visit, I was driving back home through the national park. Normally I would go via the main highway, but this time I felt like a change and wanted a bit of scenery with the drive. There were storms around and a bit of rain, but nothing to cause any concerns.

As I was nearing the end of my national park leg of the journey, I had to pass through some open heathlands. As I entered this open area I saw a lightning strike occur about 100 metres away, off to the side of the road, and heard an almighty crack of thunder. I was awestruck and couldn't believe my luck at seeing a lightning strike so close. However, just as I returned my gaze to the road ahead there was another deafening boom, an incredibly bright flash of light, and the car jumped a metre to the side. A lightning strike had occurred on the road about 10 metres in front of the car. To see a strike 100 metres away was incredible. To have one occur literally metres in front of you and drive through the spot it had struck was mind-blowing.

## Temperature Extremes

In the Central Australian deserts during winter it can get pretty cold. While setting up for our evening stargazing tours, we would often feel the temperature drop from 20 degrees half an hour before sunset to -5 degrees a mere 10 minutes after the Sun went down. Being outside at this time, I could feel my lips and face dry out from the cold minute by minute as the temperature plummeted. On these nights, people would come along to our stargazing tours wrapped in blankets, and I didn't blame them, I wished I could have had a blanket as well. But the worst part was if there was any moisture in the air as it settled on the equipment, and you, it would freeze within minutes. There were many nights when I had frozen hair and ice on my shoulders.

At the other extreme, we started doing some solar viewing during afternoons, which was an excellent way to advertise and upsell visitors to the evening tours. It was enjoyable for everyone, especially myself, as looking safely at the Sun is something everyone should do at some time in their life. It is always fascinating. But, of course, solar viewing is all well and good during the winter months, but summer in the desert is brutal. The first summer we were there the temperature in the shade on my back porch in the early afternoon was over 50 degrees for 10 days in a row. Thankfully, at night it would ease back to a balmy 38 degrees. Essentially, I turned the air-conditioning on in October and didn't turn it off until April.

Now, with these sorts of temperatures during summer, you have to take precautions, especially if you want to stand out in the sun for a couple of hours each afternoon looking through a telescope. Lots of sunscreen, long sleeve shirts, hats and shade from an umbrella were mandatory. Even so, there were days where we had to stop early because the heat was just too much. Australians know that to be out in this sort of heat unprotected for even an hour can cause death, but many tourists didn't seem to understand. There were always some to be found sunbaking beside the pool mid-afternoon in 50 degree temperatures!

## Atmosphere

One of the persistent problems for astronomers and their use of telescopes is the atmosphere. Although essential for humans to breathe, it causes nothing but problems for our view of the stars. Astronomer's call the effect the atmosphere has on the view of the heavens 'seeing'. Consequently, you may hear someone who owns a telescope talk about what the 'seeing' was like last night. To the general, non-telescope owning public, the effect is referred to as 'twinkling' when using just your eyes to look at the stars. The more a star twinkles, the worse the seeing. The less it twinkles, the better the seeing. To get the best views you need to pick a night when the seeing is not too bad.

This rapid distortion of our view is caused by the turbulent atmosphere having numerous pockets and layers of air with varying refractive indices. As the starlight passes through these different patches they make the light bend slightly in different directions and the star appears to jiggle around. Professional observatories try to minimise this problem by putting telescopes on the tops of mountains, above most of the atmosphere, or out in space where there is no atmosphere at all to get in the way.

Working at the Ayers Rock Resort in Central Australia, we were there to provide entertainment and the opportunity for people to find out a little more about the night sky. It didn't matter whether the seeing was good or bad; we just wanted to give people the chance to look through a telescope. But one night a person asked one of the most pointless questions I have ever heard. They wanted to show off that they knew a bit about astronomy, so they asked "How often do you get sub-arcsecond seeing?". This was a question about how steady the atmosphere was, which determines how much detail (or resolution) you can see. But sub-arcsecond seeing is an excessively small criterion to meet. It is a question you would ask at the best viewing locations, with the steadiest atmosphere on the planet (where the best telescopes are found for that reason), not in the middle of a desert at an altitude of only 500 metres above sea level. Conditions at that level of clarity did occasionally occur, but they existed for only ever so brief a moment. I still smile when I think about that question.

What the atmosphere carries can also be a problem. Living in Central Australia, one of the biggest threats was dust, bright red dust. It got everywhere, including on the telescope optics, no matter how careful we were. Dust on the optics diminishes the effectiveness of your telescope, so you need to keep them as clean as possible. Even worse though is scratching the optics when trying to remove the dust. As annoying as it can be, it is often better to leave some dust on the optics, providing it isn't too bad, but if you must clean it, you need to be very, very careful. Better still, give it to a professional to clean.

And it wasn't only dust that created problems for our telescopes. We had to cope with the airborne grease from the regular barbeques held 500 metres away. As a telescope owner, that shows you have to be forever vigilant, as even things you think couldn't possibly affect your telescope have to be carefully monitored.

Dew is another atmospheric problem that is the bane of all telescopes. The need to protect telescope optics from dew has spawned numerous accessories to try and cope with the problem. Dew caps, hairdryers and small heaters have all been employed. However, the best protection against dew is to not use the telescope when dew is a problem. Of course, that's not always possible, and you have to cope with the issue the best way you can.

One word of advice though, never wipe any dew off the optics. This will only scratch the optics and degrade the view through your telescope.

Everyone who has a telescope has had to deal with dew, but the most notable instance I have come across was working in The Centre. Generally, the air out there is dry, one per cent humidity during winter and 10 per cent humidity in summer was the norm. Dew was never a problem, except, for some reason, as the seasons transitioned from summer to winter. At this time there were 2 weeks where the dew was so heavy it looked as if we had hosed down the telescopes. Standing outside for just 5 minutes rendered you dripping wet. It is the only place I've been where I had to wear a waterproof jacket to keep dry on a crystal clear night. After 2 weeks, it would suddenly disappear only to reappear as we transitioned from winter back to summer when the same thing would happen again.

My sister and myself with our first, and only, pet rabbit

Getting to know the pigs on a relative's farm at Bellingen, NSW

One of the few friendly dogs I knew in my younger days

Playing with trout and lambs at a relative's fish farm near Dorrigo, NSW

Our family cat as a kitten

My mother's Blue Cattle Dog

My grandfather's Rosella that became a family pet after he died

Mum feeding the King Parrots

Lightning storm over Uluru

Water cascading off Uluru during a storm

A waterfall off Uluru

CHAPTER 9

# People With 'Interesting' Ideas

―

As anyone who has worked in the public spotlight knows, eventually you will have people with 'unique' views seek you out to discuss their 'original' thoughts. It is no different for me, and since they tag me as being the expert in all things to do with science and space, it seems they think I will understand and agree that their ideas are correct, no matter how out there they may be.

Some people I've encountered have claimed to have aliens living under their beds or been abducted by UFOs. A few even providing 'proof' by showing me photos of the sneaky extraterrestrials hiding. Of course, I could never see the aliens because they must be blocking my mind from seeing them, but I was assured they were there in the photo. It seems these people all want to know if I knew about the aliens and what they were up to, I guess simply looking for someone to validate their ideas. But since I'm not friends with any aliens and I haven't seen any spaceships, I can't do that.

There were also groups of people that, and I hesitate to use the word 'cult', held particular belief systems that I could never understand. I remember one in particular quite well.

Uluru is understandably a place of immense cultural history. In a flat landscape, the monolith stands out and immediately draws your attention, so it is no wonder it holds a special interest to anyone who sees it. Now, you may have heard of something called 'ley lines' that supposedly crisscross the globe. These are meant to be lines of energy, and where they cross is of particular importance and very influential. Apparently, these crossing points are where we find cultural artefacts, such as Stonehenge and the pyramids of Egypt. There is also meant to be one of these crossing points under Uluru, or so I am told. I have also heard that Uluru is hollow, with a spaceship hiding inside, so I don't know that I should believe everything I hear.

Anyway, early in November of 1991, a group that followed a mystic called Solaris decided to meet at Uluru and channel its energy. Their premise was that the numbers 11:11 held special significance (the reason given was "How many times have you looked at your clock, and it read 11:11?") and Solaris had convinced them that the time had come to use this. What they planned to do was get 144,000 people (again, apparently a significant number) to surround Uluru while holding hands on the first day of the 11th month of 1991 (i.e. 1/11/1991 or 1111991, don't ask me what happens with the 991 at the end) and meditate for 24 hours. They had calculated that they needed 144,000 people, although walking around the base of Uluru is just under 10 kilometres so that would mean each person had only about 7 centimetres in which to stand. Assuming a more practical spacing, if we allow half a metre for each person that means their circle of believers would be 72 kilometres around and place each person about 11½ kilometres from The Rock, which seems to me like it would be too far away to suck up any energy from the ley line. The Solaris believers apparently also did not know that the national park closed at sunset and no one was allowed to be in there overnight.

As it turns out, only a few dozen people showed up, so it wasn't an issue. Their plan may not have been successful, but they did provide a couple of days of interesting conversations as they tried to convert us.

Other people had more of a scientific agenda and wanted me to tell them their theories are correct and that they were onto something big. Working at Sydney Observatory provided the perfect opportunity for these people to find someone who will listen to them, even if it is only to be polite.

I regularly had a lady visit who would tell me each time that she was a direct descendant of Sir Isaac Newton. Not completely out of the question, except that it seems he never had sex and died a virgin. Giving her the benefit of the doubt, maybe she was mistaking the connection of simply being related through a relative of Sir Isaac as meaning 'directly descended'.

Another time at Sydney Observatory we had a group of people stay at one of our overnight camps. Normally the camps were for children, but this group was keen and managed to talk my boss into letting them have one. Their main aim was to absorb the energy from the stars overnight by looking through the telescopes and then meditate on the grass outside as the sun rose to channel the energy from the Earth.

As I was working that night, it was up to me to start the evening off by giving them a talk about space and astronomy in general. But on almost everything I mentioned I would have someone stop and question why I didn't mention some obvious spiritual aspect associated with the planet, star, or galaxy. I was trying to be polite and mention that there wasn't any evidence to support some of those ideas when someone loudly said "That's because scientists don't have any imagination and can't see the whole spectrum of ideas and possibilities that are clearly in front of them." I know I should have simply changed the subject, but the comment got under my skin a bit, so I replied that if scientists didn't have imaginations then concepts such as quantum mechanics and relativity would never have been discovered. Things would have degenerated after that except my friend stepped in and took over while I left to calm down.

Along similar lines, while working in the school boarding house, one of the boys had some peculiar ideas and would get quite aggressive if you didn't agree with him. He continually claimed that Einstein was wrong, and he could prove it. It was well known that I had a background in science, so whenever I was on duty, he would try to convince me of his ideas. As much as I tried to cut him off before he got started, he would persist and generally, I would give in, as he would get agitated if I didn't give him at least some opportunity to say something. As he mentioned specific ideas on where he thought Einstein was wrong, I would try to explain why what he said wasn't correct, but that would just make him more determined and angry. Eventually, the other boys realised what was going on and some of them would come and interrupt with a fake emergency that I had to deal with, just to get me out of the conversation.

But perhaps the most prolific person with wild scientific ideas was a gentleman by the name of Mr Thomas. Every month for years he would send to Sydney Observatory a 20 sheet, foolscap sized letter explaining his latest idea. Every sheet was double-sided and typed and each letter would outline a completely different idea from any he had previously sent. They always ended with an invitation to reply with our thoughts. It was usually impossible to follow his reasoning so replying was not an option and the letters were simply filed away. Occasionally we would read them just for amusement. It must have taken him the entire month between letters to type them up, so we figured that must be all he did.

Since all we ever received were letters, we didn't feel the need to take things too seriously, but there was one day when I had a visitor come into the observatory and start to talk about some ideas he had and asking for my opinions. After an hour or so he left and I didn't think much more about it until I told a colleague, who mentioned that the ideas sounded very familiar. The more we talked the more we realised that they were very similar to the letters we got from Mr Thomas. It seems that I had met the famous man in person. To my knowledge, he never came into the observatory again.

# Part Three
## Passion

# CHAPTER 10
# Astronomy

---

Dealing with depression for half of my life has been difficult. At times, the only way I have managed was by having something I was passionate about and immersing myself in it. It allowed me to retreat to a place where I felt comfortable and happy, even if the rest of my life felt very depressing. In my case, that place of retreat is in science, astronomy in particular, and more specifically, imparting it to the general public. For someone else, it will undoubtedly be something completely different.

But that love of science and explaining it to other people didn't suddenly spring out of thin air, it had a definite beginning.

A long time ago one of my brothers gave me a book as a birthday present. He gave me *Second Foundation* by Isaac Asimov. I was turning 11 at the time and was naturally curious about, well, everything, but until that moment I had no focus for my curiosity. Now, the third book of a trilogy was perhaps not the best one to begin with, but unknowingly my brother had picked one of the greatest science fiction stories ever written, and even though it was the last book of the series, it straight away ignited a lifelong passion for space and science. It was the right book given at the right time that sparked my imagination.

Fifty years later, I still have the book and I cannot thank my brother enough for opening that doorway for me. Needless to say, after feverishly reading *Second Foundation* I raced out and bought the first 2 books in the series and devoured them just as quickly.

A few years later, the same bother gave me a whole bunch of astronomy posters for another birthday present. At the time, besides inside a book, posters were the only way to see an image of a celestial object and I made the most of them, pinning them up on my bedroom wall for many years. I still have them all, although they are now laminated so they will last longer and be able to handle the abuse I put them through.

Looking at these images every night and reading about different celestial objects made me want to study and explore them for a living. I wanted to do more than simply read about them, I wanted to look at the real thing through a telescope. It was the reason I studied physics and mathematics at university, the reason I wanted a telescope and the reason I took the job at Sydney Observatory. Once that happened, my passion had also become my career.

The first step I needed to do was to get a decent telescope, and at the age of 16, the opportunity finally arose.

There are plenty of good telescope options out there for a reasonable price, but there is another option to consider if you are reasonably handy at building things. I am talking about the alternative of making your own telescope.

## Making A Telescope

Contrary to what you might expect, it isn't that hard to build one and make a good job of it. With a bit of patience and the following of instructions, you can grind your own mirror and assemble the telescope from its components. Building the telescope yourself has the advantage of making the completed unit slightly cheaper than an off-the-shelf telescope and that means you can generally afford to make a bigger one than you could buy ready-made. Plus, it is a great experience that allows you to more fully understand how a telescope works. The disadvantage is that although perfectly functional, they tend to be simpler than a store-bought telescope. It won't necessarily affect the optical performance, but since most people aren't engineers, it will affect the general finish, especially the mount, and may limit how you can use your instrument.

If you are prepared to put up with these limitations, or perhaps would like a big telescope but only have a small budget, then making your own telescope is a satisfying option and an adventure.

I mention this because I made a telescope myself when I was a teenager. Being obsessed with looking at the stars, I used to regularly annoy my parents to buy a telescope for me, but I was one of 5 children and my parents never had much spare money for something like a telescope. After years of pestering, my parents must have realised that my interest wasn't going to go away, so, in a moment of genius, for my 16th birthday they did the next best thing to buying a telescope, they bought me the mirror blanks and accessories to grind my own 20 centimetre diameter mirror. Grinding a mirror was a new experience for all of us. No one knew what to do or what to expect, but I had a book that explained everything, so, as only a teenager can do, I figured it couldn't be that hard.

A telescope mirror is ground by rubbing 2 thick, flat pieces of special glass over each other. The bottom piece of glass is fixed to a table and you rub the centre of the top glass over the outer part of the bottom glass. In between the two is a coarse grit that wears the glass away. After a little while, you turn everything a bit and repeat, this time rubbing different areas of both bits of glass. After doing this for hours and hours and hours, you change to a finer grit and repeat, for hours and hours and hours. You then switch to an even finer grit and repeat the process yet again.

Teenagers aren't renowned for their patience and I have to admit that at times I struggled to keep going. But slowly and surely the outside of the bottom glass gets worn away, creating a convex shape, and the centre of the top piece is worn away to create a concave surface. As the grit gets finer, the surfaces become smoother until eventually, you have concave and convex pieces of glass that are incredibly smooth. You then throw away the convex one (unless you need a paperweight) as it is now useless. You keep the concave glass as it is now your telescope mirror. It still needs a reflective coating applied to turn it into a proper mirror, but essentially the mirror has been made.

The mirror is, of course, just one part of a telescope. I still needed to buy the tube and other bits and pieces. It took a while to save the money, but eventually, I had all the necessary bits to complete the telescope. I painted the tube, drilled holes, measured focal lengths and finally put together my first telescope. I next turned my attention to making the mount. It wasn't pretty when I finished, and it certainly wasn't a great piece of engineering, but it worked, and it allowed me to use my very own telescope I had built from scratch.

The whole process was such a satisfying experience that 40 plus years later, I still have that telescope. It works, but I haven't used it for many years. The homemade mount fell apart a long time ago, and since then, I have had several commercially made telescopes, so I don't have any need for it anymore. But I can't bear to get rid of it, so it now sits in the sunroom as a piece of artwork in the corner.

That first telescope gave me an enormous amount of enjoyment and allowed me to discover things I had only ever read about or seen on my posters.

**Finding Planets**

I think it is safe to say that the very first thing anyone looks at when they get a telescope for the first time is the Moon, and I was no different. It is easy to locate and has a wealth of detail to explore. With craters and mountains galore, there is always something to look at. Throw in the darker flat areas known as 'seas' and you can try and find the landing places of each of the Apollo spacecraft. Each month the Moon goes through a series of phases and occasionally it passes into the Earth's shadow to create a lunar eclipse. Although easy to see and often ignored because of it, the Moon is one of the most fascinating objects in the sky to look at.

But, as I was growing up, I use to look into a clear night sky and wonder if any of the twinkling points of light might be planets. I wanted to find them and use my telescope to look at them. Like most people, I wanted to find the big ones, Saturn and Jupiter, but the one I most wanted to see was elusive Mercury. Don't ask me why, I just did.

I spent hours trying to identify them. My method of planet hunting was sound, or at least it was in the mind of a teenager, as I had read somewhere that stars twinkle and planets don't, so I figured if I looked around the sky for a point of light that wasn't twinkling, then that would be a planet. Sadly, I had been led astray. Everything twinkles, including the planets, so I never did find any of them until years later when I learnt how to locate them correctly.

So, if twinkling status won't do it, how can you tell which point of light is a planet and which is a star? Few printed star maps will have the planets marked on them because they move so fast compared to the stars. If you were to mark the planets on your map, it would only be suitable for that year. Leave them off, and the star map is good for a thousand years. So, star maps are out if you want to find the planets.

The word 'planet' comes from the Greek for 'wandering star' since the planets move compared to the background stars. So, another way to find a planet is to pick a point of light in the sky, watch it for a month or 2 and see if it moves compared to the stars. If it does, chances are it is a planet. If it doesn't, pick another one. Alternatively, you could narrow down your search by looking up which constellation the planet is meant to be in and once again pick a bright point of light within the constellation, watch it for a month or 2 and see if it moves compared to the stars. If it doesn't, pick another one. Obviously, this approach takes a lot of patience.

The way to confirm you have found a planet is to look at it with a telescope, or in a pinch, a good pair of binoculars. Through even the biggest telescope in the world, a single star will look like a pinpoint of light. But through any telescope, no matter what size, a planet will show a disc. It may not be a big disc, but it will definitely be more than a pinpoint and tell you definitively that it is a planet, not a star.

It was this last method I used after building my telescope. Work out a reasonable candidate somehow, then confirm if it is, or isn't, a planet by using the telescope.

An easier way these days would be to use a program or an app that tells you when a particular planet is visible and where to look. You can also then use an app to check whether you have the right point of light, but that somewhat defeats the satisfaction and sense of achievement you get from being able to locate it for yourself.

Whichever way you choose to locate them, Venus and Jupiter are the easiest to find. They are the brightest points of light in the night sky after the Moon. Everyone who has ever looked up at night will have seen them, whether they knew what they were looking at or not.

Saturn is not quite as bright as Venus or Jupiter. It just looks like a bright yellowish star, but if you know where to look, it is easy enough to see. The same with Mars, although it is even easier as it has a distinctive reddish hue to it.

But with Mercury, the remaining naked eye visible planet, very few people have ever seen it or at least realised that's what it was. Since Mercury never appears far from the Sun, it tends to be lost in the Sun's glare most of the time. It is, however, visible for brief periods throughout the year just after sunset or before sunrise when it appears at its greatest distance (called Greatest Elongation) from the Sun.

That leaves Uranus and Neptune to complete the set. Unfortunately, there is no getting around the fact that you need a telescope to see these two.

It took me a few years from those first attempts as a 16 year old with a homemade telescope, but I have now seen all 7 planets in our solar system (8 if you count the Earth) and know how to find them whenever I want.

With the individual planets and their surface details seen with a telescope, the next challenge was to look for other interesting things associated with each of them.

Our Moon is not the only moon in the solar system. Most planets have at least one moon, the only exceptions being Mercury and Venus. Jupiter has 4 easy ones to see, even a small telescope will show them to you. They were first discovered by Galileo in the early 1600s and the telescope he used was smaller and nowhere near as good quality as a modern pair of binoculars. The moons of Saturn are almost as easy, with 9 of the brightest ones visible with a moderate-sized telescope. Uranus and Neptune need something a little bigger in order to see their moons, but they are possible. The only planetary moons that still elude me are the 2 tiny rocks orbiting Mars. The biggest is only 11 kilometres across, so it is no wonder it poses such a difficult challenge when the closest the planet comes to the Earth is still about 62 million kilometres away.

The other challenge I set myself was to try and see the planets during the daytime. I've seen Mercury, Mars, Jupiter and Saturn, but each requires a telescope to locate and see.

If you know where to look, Venus is the only planet visible during the day using just your eyes. But finding it without some guide to its location is extremely difficult, as your eyes have trouble focusing on a point of light against the bright blue background. The best way to locate it is to find out when Venus will be close to the Moon and use the Moon to determine where in the sky Venus should be. A handy tip is to wear sunglasses, as they do help to dull the bright blue sky. Once found, you will wonder how you ever missed it. The first time you see Venus during the day using just your eyes is always an exciting moment, so it is worth attempting.

**Planetary Alignments**

Occasionally, some of the planets will appear close together in the sky. If they are really close we call them planetary alignments, although, generally it is more like a close grouping than an actual alignment.

Some people seem obsessed with planetary alignments. Of course, some are keen amateur astronomers with an interest in seeing all the planets in one night, but others think that the planets aligning will bring on the end of the world. Is there any way an alignment of the planets could significantly affect the Earth? The short answer is no.

In everyday use, when things are 'aligned' they are said to be in the same orientation, and their centres are precisely lined up. If we apply this definition to the planets, it would mean all 8 planets would be hiding perfectly behind each other. Alignments between just 2 planets occur very rarely, so alignments between 3 or more planets are much rarer still.

Momentarily forgetting that the planets don't all go around the Sun in the same plane, so can't possibly line up behind each other, let's assume the planets could line up perfectly. How strong would the combined gravitational influence of the planets be on the Earth?

Mighty Jupiter only pulls on the Earth about one per cent as hard as the Moon. Venus is next with only 0.6 per cent of the Moon's force. If we add them up, the total pull of all the planets combined is still only 1.7 per cent of the Moon's pull. That isn't much, but is it enough to destroy the Earth? The Moon orbits the Earth in an ellipse. That means it is closer to the Earth sometimes than at other times. At perigee, or closest approach, it is about 363,000 kilometres away and at apogee, or farthest point, it is about 405,000 kilometres away. Because of this, the Moon's gravitational effect on the Earth fluctuates by about 25 per cent each orbit. The Moon orbits the Earth in about a month, going from apogee to perigee every 2 weeks. So, every 14 days we experience a change in gravitational effect from the Moon more than 10 times greater than all the planets combined.

So, if gravity won't render the Earth in two, what about the tidal effect of the planets?

Since the tidal force is related to distance, the close approaches between Venus and Earth are the most critical factor in determining the combined planetary tide on Earth. The point at which the Venus tide is at a maximum corresponds to a tidal acceleration that is 1/10,000 as strong as the Sun's average tidal acceleration on Earth and over 20,000 times smaller than the tidal acceleration induced twice every day by the Moon.

Since they never happen, let's forget about exact alignments and talk about close groupings of the planets.

For the planets Mercury through to Saturn, as viewed from Earth, in the period between 3100 BCE and 2750 CE the last relatively close alignment was in May 2000, where they were within 20 degrees of each other. I remember looking at it and being suitably impressed at the time.

Within this almost 6,000 year period, however, 55 alignments are at least as close as the one of May 2000. This means, on average close alignments occur about 9 times every 1,000 years. Before 2000 CE, the last alignment that was as close occurred in February 1962 CE. If we look at the closest alignment during this period, it happened in late February 1953 BCE when they were just 4 degrees apart. That would have been a spectacular sight. The next alignment of note occurs around 8 September 2040 CE when they will be 8 degrees apart. That is not as wide as your closed fist held at arm's length. Make sure you put this date in your diary as you will not want to miss it.

Mercury is moderately hard to see from the Earth, so what if we take Mercury out of the list and look at the remaining planets you can see with the unaided eye, that is, Venus through to Saturn. The closest alignment in the period stated above will be in February 2378 CE with a width of just 3 degrees. Incidentally, the last big one was in June 1564 CE at 4 degrees separation.

## Non-Planetary Solar System

The planets are great, but perhaps my most favourite object to look at is the Sun. It is very dangerous to do so, but if you use the right equipment, the view of our closest star is always fascinating. Details such as sunspots, flares and prominences are easily seen through solar filters and are forever changing. Explaining this to people and pointing out the features visible as they look through the telescope is one way to get me super enthusiastic about the universe around us.

Living in a large city doesn't matter when looking at the Sun, but it does tend to make some objects either invisible or, at best, extremely difficult to see. So, the first time I visited a truly dark location and looked at the sky I was amazed. Seeing the Milky Way in all its glory for the first time was wonderful and I still enjoy just lying on my back and gazing at it.

Incidentally, if you are in a really dark location, then not long after sunset or before sunrise you might also notice what looks like a second Milky Way reaching up from the horizon. Our galaxy isn't splitting itself in half, instead, you are looking at something known as the Zodiacal Light. The solar system is full of fine dust particles which scatter the Sun's light. This scattered light is very faint so it is easily drowned out by moonlight or light pollution, which is why it can only be seen from a dark location. Since the dust is in the same plane as the planets and the planets only pass through the Zodiac constellations, this scattered light can only be found along the zodiac as well, hence its name.

**Meteors**

If you are lying outside looking at the Milky Way, it is also possible to notice that there are lots of meteors visible all night long. Meteors are bits of dust and small rocks from space colliding with the Earth at enormous speeds. As they crash into the atmosphere, they make the air around them extremely hot, melting the meteor and causing a bright streak across the sky before vaporising completely and disappearing. Meteors can be fast or slow, faint or bright, brief or long depending on all manner of things, such as the angle they enter the atmosphere, or whether they are catching up to the Earth in its orbit or running headlong into it. Occasionally a larger meteor, maybe the size of your fist, will collide with the Earth and produce an extra bright display. These are known as fireballs.

As you can imagine, the sudden appearance of a bright light streaking across the sky at enormous speeds then suddenly disappearing could cause concern, especially if it lasts for more than a second or two. I have had many phone calls about spacecraft flying across the sky, displaying aerial acrobatics and then suddenly zooming off so fast they disappear.

Sometimes I've been lucky enough to see the same event and realise it was just a meteor.

If you have ever been to the Ayers Rock Resort in Central Australia, you know that even from the centre of the resort, with all its lights, the view of the night sky is truly spectacular. While I was working there, part of the evening tour I conducted involved pointing out the stars and constellations using just our eyes. We were under one of the wonders of nature, the dark night sky, and the last thing we needed was light, as this wrecks your night vision and upsets the view. One night, I had just finished pointing out a constellation and looked down at the group when suddenly there was an extremely bright flash of light. A second later, there was another. Then another. My first thought was that someone in the group was taking multiple photos using a flash. I was about to ask them to stop when I noticed everyone was looking up, so I did too. What we were witnessing was a rare fireball coming almost straight down at us. As it came through the atmosphere bits of it broke off, and these bits created the bright flashes as they vaporised. If you didn't know a meteor could do that, what we had seen could have easily been misidentified as an alien UFO.

On another night, we were looking at a crystal clear sky when a slow-moving object appeared and for a count of about 40 (which is an exceptionally long time) travelled across almost the entire sky. This was probably a meteor or piece of space junk skipping off the upper atmosphere before heading back out into space. These are not uncommon, but you have to be lucky to see them.

**Comets**

In 1973, my first year of high school, I convinced about 8 of my new school friends to stay over one night to see another type of temporary object in the sky. Known as Comet Kohoutek, it would be my very first comet, and since it was advertised as the comet of the century, I was excited. The problem was that, according to the news, the comet was only going to be visible in the early hours of the morning. Being 12 at the time meant, of course, we just had to stay up all night.

The next problem was that the news, where we heard about the comet and got our information from, was very light on details about how to find it and what time to start looking. The time problem didn't faze us because we knew we were going to stay up all night, so whenever it was visible, we would be ready. But none of us knew the sky well enough to know where to look. I now know that the place where we searched was completely wrong, but perhaps the most significant problem was that it didn't live up to expectations and was a lot fainter than predicted. Oh, for the internet back then!

In later life, this experience taught me that when giving details about comets and how to see them, I made sure to provide information that even the most astronomically untrained person could follow.

Having said that, one time I perhaps didn't explain myself as clearly as I could, or should, have.

I was working at Sydney Observatory and we were experiencing an extended period of clear, stable weather and a comet was faintly visible to the west for a short period immediately after sunset. I can't remember the name of the comet as it wasn't particularly spectacular or well-known. One day, about lunchtime, long before it would be visible, a gentleman called to enquire about the comet. He thought he saw it the night before and wanted to check if that was what he had seen. He explained where and when he saw the object and I told him it could have been the comet but to have a look again that night. Comets tend to move little from night to night, especially the fainter, further from the Earth ones. If he saw it in the same position at the same time it would confirm it was the comet and not something else.

Anyone familiar with looking at the sky and comets in particular, will perhaps see my mistake. Because the initial phone call was in the middle of the day, I couldn't confirm his sighting by looking out the window. The next day he rang again, this time later in the day, saying he could see it right now and to thank me for the information. This time, I was able to look out the window and as soon as I did, I realised what he was looking at was not the comet but the condensation trail from a plane. I had not given it a thought that the weather at that time was conducive to planes creating trails and that at the same time every afternoon the same flight would take the same flight path, meaning each afternoon at the same time in the same location in the sky there would be a contrail. I immediately told him it wasn't the comet, but he would have none of that. He said I had told him if he saw it again the following night at the same time and the same location then it was the comet. No matter how much I apologised for my mistake, he refused to believe me. To this day he probably still thinks it was the comet he saw.

In 1986 I was involved with my first major astronomical event. Halley's Comet had returned, and the world was abuzz with excitement. Remembering Comet Kohoutek a decade earlier, I had learnt my lesson and was determined to make sure everyone knew where and when and what to look for. We all knew Halley's Comet was never going to be as spectacular as it was the last time it had appeared in 1910, but that didn't stop the media from going berserk. It did, however, teach me my first couple of working life media lessons. Firstly, it doesn't matter what you say, the media will edit whatever it is to the point where it is totally out of context. Secondly, they will only use seconds of the interview. To avoid these problems, you need to develop the art of getting your point across in 5 second soundbites.

Even though I knew what to expect from the comet, Halley was my first major one since Kohoutek so I was excited, but at the time a lot of people were disappointed. They were expecting the apparition hyped-up by the media, and it was never going to be that. The thing to keep in mind, and I said it many times while it was visible, is how many bright comets have you seen? Since Halley, there have been only a handful bright enough to see using only your eyes. Halley may not have been as big as some people expected, but it was easily visible from my backyard in a light-polluted suburb of Sydney.

Halley was not the only comet I was involved with on a professional basis. In mid-1994, an event occurred that took the entire world by surprise. A comet was discovered that had passed a little too close to Jupiter and was torn apart by its massive gravitational field. It had produced a string of cometary fragments that had been calculated to crash into Jupiter on its next pass. No one knew what to expect. Would the impacts be visible, or would we see nothing? Would it be a public relations nightmare or boon? The difficulty with any new astronomical event is it is difficult to predict what, if anything, will be visible. Comets, in particular, are notoriously fickle for this. What would be seen when one crashed into Jupiter was anybody's guess.

The difficulty we had at Sydney Observatory, therefore, was just how much we invested in both time and advertising in the event. Given the one-off nature of the experience, we eventually decided to go all out and hold a major event where people could come and see Jupiter on each of the predicted 6 nights of impact. It was the correct decision, as things turned out spectacularly well. The weather co-operated brilliantly, all 6 nights were crystal clear, and Jupiter was in the perfect position to look at all evening.

Given the publicity the comet impact was generating we were expecting maybe a few hundred visitors per evening. And since we had advertised we would only be open for 4 hours each night, we felt we needed everyone working in order to get whoever showed up through in that time. Altogether there were 32 full-time, part-time and casual staff working each evening.

To keep everyone who came along occupied, all the staff had specific jobs. Usually, we collected entry fees inside the building, but for this event, we put a table down at the front gate so we didn't clog things up with people trying to pay inside. That required 2 staff. We had talks running continually in the theatre. That occupied 2 more staff, who alternated between giving the talk and crowd control for the people waiting outside the theatre. Three more staff wandered around the exhibition space, helping wherever they could. Five people were on general crowd control and answered questions outside with the telescopes. Two people did nothing but circulate between the different stations, running errands, delivering messages and providing relief for staff that needed to go to the bathroom. One person was in charge, making decisions and securing money collected from entry fees. But perhaps the best decision we made was to have 2 people assigned to do nothing specific, just floating around doing anything they saw needed to be done and alerting the appropriate staff if they saw potential problems arising. Everyone else operated the 2 large telescopes in the observatory's domes as well as 5 smaller telescopes in the yard of the observatory. If it sounds like it was busy, it was.

On the first night, we were ready to open at twilight. Already we could see there was a queue outside the gate, but we didn't appreciate just how long it was. As the night set in, we realised our estimate of a few hundred people per night was a dramatic underestimate. There was always a queue out the gate, at times about 400 metres long stretching to the bottom of the hill. Four hours was never going to be enough for the number we had and by the time we closed that first night, we had counted over 1,000 people had come through the gates and it was 2 am in the morning.

I lived about 40 minutes away, so by the time I got home and crashed into bed, it was about 3 am. By itself, this wouldn't have been a problem except that I had to be back at work by 10 am, which meant leaving home at 9 am. Five hours of sleep was barely enough to recover.

The first night was a portent of what was to come. Every night we would start at 6 pm, at twilight, and finish around 2 am. Every day I would have to be back at work by 10 am and do it all again. By the end of the 6 nights, I was so tired I was working on autopilot. It was exhausting, but one of the best working weeks I have ever had.

All up, over the 6 nights, approximately 6,000+ people visited the observatory to watch Comet Shoemaker-Levy 9 crash into Jupiter. Amazingly there were only minor issues, and I put that down to the organisation and resources we had put into every evening. As a bonus, the entry fees taken were enough for the observatory to buy a new telescope and some other equipment we needed.

The view through the telescopes was spectacular and we found the best view was at the very beginning of the evening, during twilight. At that time the seeing was a lot steadier, and because the sky was still a bit light there was less contrast between Jupiter and the background, so it made the detail on the planet easier to see. The impacts themselves occurred just out of sight around the edge of Jupiter. Fortunately, it was on the side that soon rotated into view, so we didn't have to wait long to see the aftermath. On the first night, we anxiously watched to see if anything would be visible and lo and behold a black spot about the size of the Earth rotated into view. Each night as we set up we excitedly looked to see what had happened in the last 16 hours and we were never disappointed. A new spot, or 2, would be visible and by the end of the week, there was a line of spots circling Jupiter. These then hung around for a few weeks.

Since Shoemaker-Levy 9 there have been other comets, but I have tried to make sure I wasn't working when they were best visible, as I wanted to make sure I did not have any interruptions and could enjoy them myself.

**Satellites**

Other, more regularly visible objects are some of the thousands of satellites now in orbit around the Earth. Some can be seen from here on the Earth's surface. For example, if you know when and where to look the Hubble Space Telescope and the International Space Station can be easily seen regularly. They appear as bright, star-like objects moving across the sky at a steady pace and are visible for only about an hour or so after the Sun sets. It may be getting dark down here, but up where they are the Sun is still shining. That means the sky is getting darker, making them easier to see, and they appear brighter as they reflect the sunlight down to us.

As the evening progresses, the satellites may not be visible the whole way across the sky. They travel partway across before winking out as they enter the Earth's shadow and no longer reflect sunlight. Sometimes they can pulse brightly as they tumble in their orbit. Occasionally they will suddenly flare up as they reflect the light perfectly back to you, returning to normal brightness as the angle between the satellite and your location changes. Lately, there are trains of satellites in orbit and these appear like a string of pearls moving across the sky. If ever there was an alien spacecraft sighting waiting to happen, this is it. Given how many satellites there are in the train, the 'aliens' look like they are swarming, getting ready for an invasion.

## Stellar Distances

Further afield, when I look at the posters my brother gave me, I notice they are all objects outside of the Solar System. Comprising open star clusters, globular star clusters, nebulae, and galaxies, it is a veritable who's who of celestial wonders and became my initial list of things to find in the sky. Ultimately, one of them became my most favourite object to view. Visible faintly to the naked eye even from the city, Omega Centauri, the best globular cluster in the sky, is truly spectacular when seen from a dark location through a telescope. It never ceases to amaze me and is usually the first thing I look at with the telescope, if it is visible, to make sure I start the evening's viewing on a positive note.

I may have had my beginners list to find and look at, but initially, I struggled to locate any of them, at least until I realised there were no shortcuts and I had to learn my way around the night sky. Not only that, but I had to understand why things change. Questions like why do the stars move from east to west throughout the night, why are the stars and

Moon in slightly different positions at the same time each night, why do we have seasons, and why does the length of twilight vary depending on your latitude, were just some that needed to be answered before I could successfully locate all of my wish list.

This last one helped me explain an observation I had while sitting on the beach at the tip of Cape York. Being the most northerly point of mainland Australia meant I was well and truly in the tropics, and as I sat there, watching the sunset, I was amazed at how quickly it got dark. I was used to civil twilight lasting for around 30 minutes, but at Cape York, it only lasted about 10 minutes before the stars became easily visible. Incidentally, I had my first ever glimpse of the small, faint Andromeda Galaxy from that beach just minutes after the Sun went below the horizon.

In case you were wondering, Civil Twilight is defined as the period in the morning and the evening when the centre of the Sun is 6 degrees below the horizon. These are the limits at which light is still sufficient to distinguish objects. At this point, you would have to turn on the lights if you are having a bar-b-que outside. Nautical Twilight is when the centre of the Sun is 12 degrees below the horizon. At this point, you can no longer distinguish the horizon out at sea. And Astronomical Twilight is when the centre of the Sun is 18 degrees below the horizon and there is no scattered sunlight at all visible.

In the tropics, the Sun is higher in the sky during the day and consequently hits the horizon at a steep angle. The centre of the sun, therefore, gets to 6 degrees below the horizon, and hence the end of civil twilight, reasonably quickly. The further you are from the equator, the lower the Sun is in the sky and it strikes the horizon at a shallower angle. Since it takes longer to get to six degrees below the horizon, civil twilight lasts longer.

As my expertise in finding my way around the sky and locating objects of increasing faintness improved, I managed to add to my list of objects viewed through the telescope. Dwarf planets Pluto and Ceres, asteroids Pallas and Vesta, and distant galaxies have now all been seen.

But perhaps one object I will only see once in my lifetime was a naked eye visible supernova.

Roughly 163,000 years ago a star named Sanduleak -69°202 decided it was time to self-destruct. It blew itself apart and although the explosion took place long ago, the star resided in the Large Magellanic Cloud, so the light didn't reach us until the 24th of February 1987 CE. The supernova, known as SN1987A, was the brightest death of a star seen from the Earth since the supernova recorded by Johannes Kepler in 1604 CE. That star, however, was in our galaxy, a mere 20,000 light-years away.

Simply stated, a supernova occurs when a star's fuel supply driving its fusion reactions has been exhausted. Without the outward pressure generated by the energy at its centre, gravity takes over, and the star rapidly collapses in on itself and then explodes cataclysmically. SN1987A brightened in just 3 hours, faded and then took almost 3 months to reach its maximum. It wasn't until May, 80 days after its discovery, that SN1987A attained its peak brightness. At its peak it was easily visible from the centre of Sydney and if you knew where to point a telescope, visible during the daytime.

At the time the supernova occurred, I was working at Sydney Observatory, which lies on the northern side of the city. That meant to see the supernova we had to look over the bright city skyline. Even so, the night after we heard of the supernova, a few of us walked out into the grounds of the observatory, looked south and there it was. We did not have to search for it or use a telescope. It stood out easily in an otherwise empty patch of sky devoid of fainter stars due to the city lights. It was quite exciting and, ultimately, we were able to see the supernova, with just our eyes, for quite a few months.

I hope I get to see another naked-eye supernova in my lifetime but, unfortunately, I don't know that I should hold my breath over it.

## Transits

A rare event that I have been lucky enough to see more than once is the transit of Venus across the surface of the Sun. I've now seen it twice and know that I won't get to see it again. Back in 2004 CE and 2012 CE, Venus passed directly between the Earth and the Sun and we had the view of Venus moving across the Sun's disc over several hours. Unfortunately, we will now have to wait until the year 2117 CE before we see Venus do it again.

Venus, however, is not the only planet to put on a show with the Sun, as Mercury also transits the solar disc. Thankfully a lot more often than

Venus does. I have now seen Mercury transit the Sun 5 times.

Transits don't occur every time Mercury and Venus move between the Sun and the Earth because their orbits are tilted slightly to ours, and most of the time they appear to pass above or below the solar disc. But fortunately, the Sun appears quite big to us, so the alignment doesn't have to be perfect and consequently transits of either planet aren't that rare.

The only other celestial body to transit the Sun from here on Earth is the Moon, although technically when the Moon is involved, we call it an eclipse rather than a transit. I have yet to see a total eclipse of the Sun but I have been fortunate enough to see a number of partial solar eclipses. Although total solar eclipses occur somewhere in the world on a regular basis (so I guess, like a lot of people I could travel to see one), it turns out I don't have to wait much longer to have one come to me. When the Moon lies directly between the Earth and Sun its shadow falls onto the Earth. If you happen to lie under this shadow the Moon completely blocks out the Sun and it goes dark. Fortunately, for me, the next time the Moon's shadow falls directly over my house is on 22nd July 2028. For any one particular spot on the Earth, there is a total solar eclipse every 375 years, so hopefully, the weather is clear!

**Public Observatory**

Discovering things for myself is always fulfilling, but explaining what I have learnt to other people is an equal part of my passion.

Working for someone else makes life easier, but running your own business dedicated to science communication is a lot more satisfying. At the Ayers Rock Resort, I had my first opportunity to do both when I established, with a friend, a public observatory amongst the sand dunes.

Running your own business is tough. In the beginning, you don't have a lot of resources or money, and your time is 100 per cent devoted to establishing yourself. If it is your first business, it is doubly hard. Moving out to Central Australia and establishing a profitable public observatory in an already thriving resort was both a blessing and a challenge. It was a blessing because they already had marketing systems in place, plus an established visitor base. It was a challenge for the same reasons. It meant we had to slot into this existing system immediately while establishing our business.

Aside from the stress of continuously working, living in the Centre was great. The lifestyle and people were relaxed and friendly, the stargazing was amazing, and the experiences were incredible. We occasionally managed to sneak in some sightseeing, going to places only the locals knew, plus we got to meet some wonderful visitors.

When we moved out of our temporary location in the resort's amphitheatre and onto a purpose-built deck, something we didn't anticipate when designing the observatory was the number of amateur astronomers who said we should have built domes for the telescopes, rather than open decks. We couldn't understand this as we had specifically opted for an open deck plan in order to be under one of the great natural wonders, a truly dark night sky. The last thing we wanted was to be inside a dome. It may have been better for the telescopes, although that was debatable, but from an experiential perspective, being under the open sky was the only way to go.

Another thing that took me by surprise occurred when the construction of our new platform was nearing completion. Talks turned to the signage to be placed at the start of each track leading across the dunes to our new home. The resort wanted to know what we wanted on the wooden signs. We said our name was Southern Skies Observatory so, of course, that's what should be on the sign. The resort, however, had the idea that the word 'observatory' meant a bird or animal observation deck and therefore our name would confuse people and no one would know we were looking at the stars.

I can understand how the word observatory can be used to reference a bird viewing platform, but I thought everyone knew that an observatory was what you called a place with telescopes. But apparently not. It took a while, but we eventually got the signs we wanted. I still have those signs, proudly hanging in my back yard as it was part of our deal when we left that we got to keep them.

During the time we were out there, the resort had a turnover of 7,000 visitors per night during peak times and around 5,000 during off-peak times. For us, that meant a never-ending stream of new people. It blew our minds the first time a visitor from Europe said that someone they met while backpacking in Germany had told them they must come to see us. We were internationally famous! At least that's how we ran it in our heads.

Truth be told, it may have only happened a few times, but as far as we were concerned our fame had spread worldwide.

Incidentally, our fame in Central Australia led to another strange coincidence, this time in my adopted hometown of Orange, NSW. At the time, Ronald McDonald House was in the process of fundraising for a new facility in Orange. The chairperson of the committee asked if I would be willing to help out. She said she wanted to reproduce here in Orange something she had done a number of years ago while visiting Uluru. While in The Centre she had attended a dinner in the middle of the sand dunes under the stars. At the end of the dinner, an astronomer gave a star talk and she loved it so much she wanted to recreate the same thing here. I couldn't let the opportunity pass so I asked what year she had been in the Centre and, lo and behold, it was when I was out there. It turned out my business partner had given the talk she attended. When I told her she was talking to the person who had started those dinner star talks she was super excited, so how could I not help out. She was even more excited when I said I would get my partner, who had given the talk she remembered from so long ago, to come from Sydney to help out.

The very first of these Ronald McDonald House events was held outside at one of the local wineries. The night was spectacular except for a slight problem. It was winter. When the Sun went down the temperature plummeted to zero, probably less, and people were at risk of hypothermia. The tables were set for a formal dinner, but the decision was made to move everything inside. It was quite a sight to see the guests in their black-tie outfits pick up the tables and carry everything inside the warmer building. Ultimately, we only ventured outside long enough to do the star talk before adjourning back inside with the warmth and the wine.

Fame hasn't been restricted to just word of mouth. There has been a never-ending stream of radio, newspaper and magazine interviews, as well as appearing in a diverse range of publications across the country. Throughout my entire working life I have been involved with the media and producing publications. The following is a brief list of highlights.

- Author of *One Star by Day, Six Thousand by Night: Discovering the Universe*, a book on general astronomy for the science novice
- Appeared on and provided information for numerous travel and science shows, radio programs, newspapers and TV news, about

astronomical events and the Orange Planetarium
- Created star maps used in the yearly publication *Sydney Observatory Almanac*
- Special event astronomy segments on 105.1 2MMM
- Weekly astronomy segment on 105.1 2MMM
- Weekly astronomy articles in the Central Western Daily newspaper
- Astronomical images used in the *Sydney Observatory Almanac* and as part of the permanent exhibition in Sydney Observatory
- Recorded interview on astronomy for QANTAS Radio
- Fortnightly articles for the Central Australian newspaper
- Recorded series of talks for ABC Regional Radio Alice Springs on astronomical events
- Co-authored the *Sydney Observatory Almanac*
- Sydney Observatory flyers advertising activities held for school holiday programs
- Article for *Sydney's Child* magazine about Sydney Observatory

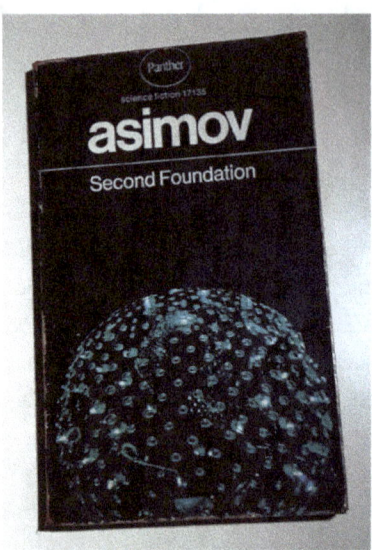

My original copy of *Second Foundation* by Isaac Asimov

A proud owner and his first telescope

My first telescope now sits in the corner of the sunroom

The full moon

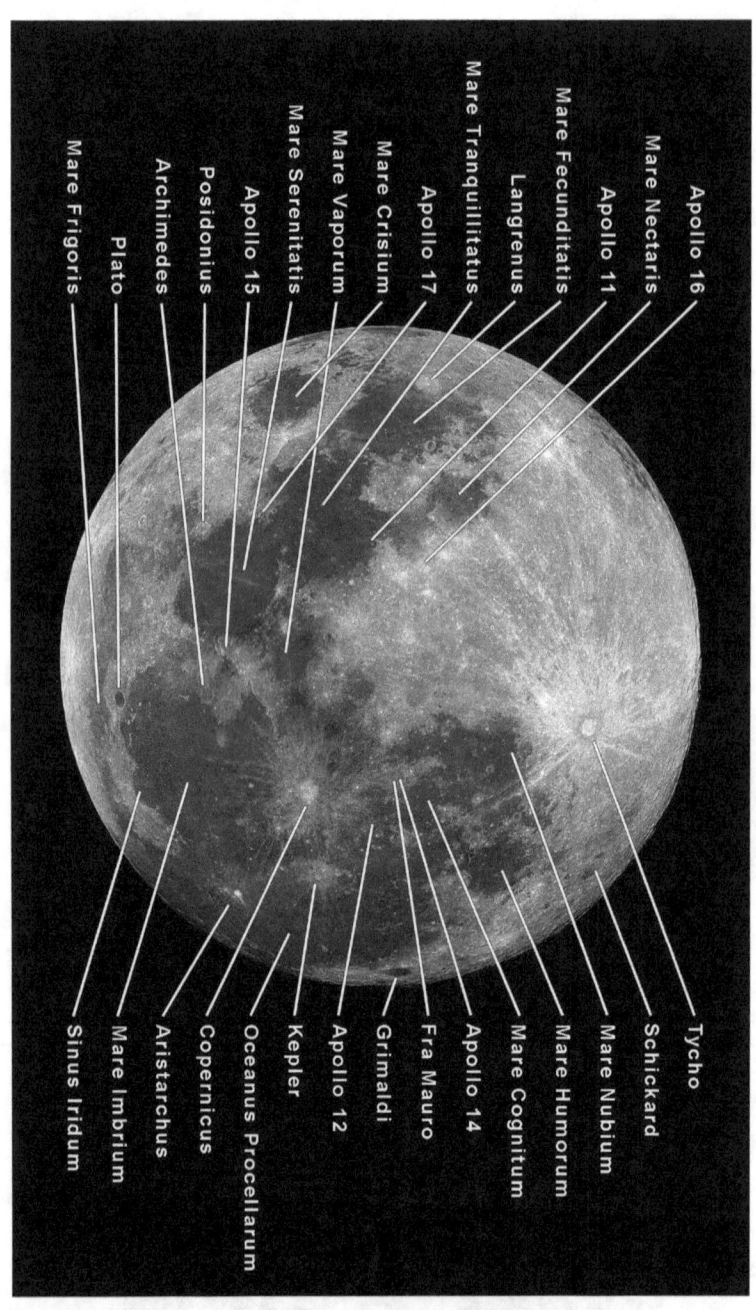

Features on the moon

Earthshine on the Moon

Lunar eclipse diagram

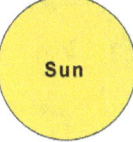 

A partial lunar eclipse

A crescent Venus minutes before it passed in front of the sun in 2012

Jupiter and 3 moons

Saturn

A planetary conjunction in 2005

A planetary conjunction in 2011

Comet Shoemaker-Levy 9 viewing at Sydney Observatory

Omega Centauri, the best globular cluster in the sky

Centaurus A galaxy

The Large Magellanic Cloud galaxy

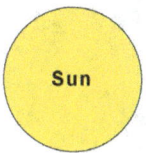 

Solar eclipse diagram

A partial solar eclipse

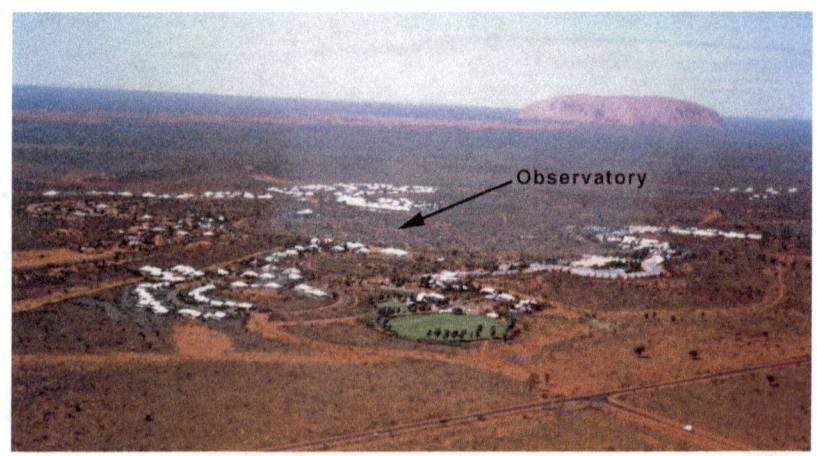

Yulara and our observatory location

Our viewing platforms amongst the sand dunes

Our observatory with Uluru in the distance

Telescopes on the viewing deck

Observatory sign at the start of a track

The same sign now lives in my back yard

Waiting to be interviewed in the cold morning air

Being interviewed for a travel show

## CHAPTER 11
# Unidentified Flying Objects

―

Before we go any further, I need to get something out of the way. Do I believe in UFOs? Yes. Do I think they're due to alien activity? No.

Don't get me wrong. I would love to have an alien spacecraft land in my backyard, although, to fit they would have to be tiny aliens in a tiny spacecraft. To be the person who has the first contact with an extraterrestrial being would be amazing, but sadly I don't think it is likely to happen. Neither do I believe it has happened to anyone else.

I have included this discussion about UFOs because if you spend much time looking at the night sky then at some point, you will see something that seems out of the ordinary.

But apart from that, I think talking about UFOs is an excellent way to excite people about science. It is natural to be fascinated by the prospect of alien life and the possibility it may be visiting us. Admittedly some people get a little carried away, but most have a healthy interest, and that can lead them into a deeper understanding of science.

By discussing why and how aliens might get here, you can introduce an audience to Astronomy and Physics. Considering the possibility of extraterrestrial life and where it might be is an excellent way of introducing people to Biology. And exploring possible explanations for UFOs introduces some Earth Sciences and Human Psychology.

To counter the growing, and dangerous, anti-science mentality in today's society, we need to increase the general scientific knowledge of the population. Too many decision-makers are ignorant of how the world works. Also, the advancement of science depends on public funding and people receiving scientific educations that enable them to make informed decisions. For me, it is a natural fit to use the interest in UFOs to introduce them to the wonders that science reveals about the real universe.

Needless to say, I have encountered more than my fair share of people claiming to have seen a UFO. Rather than dismissing them offhand, I have tried to use it to extend their knowledge of science, so, let's spend one final chapter talking about the subject.

There are many reasons why it is improbable for the Earth to have been visited by ET and there are reasonable psychological explanations as to why people believe they have seen or been abducted by aliens. But for the time being, I have a few questions to ponder over, so let's assume aliens are visiting the Earth.

Firstly, humans are a very young technological civilisation, so if aliens are visiting Earth, it is reasonable to assume they would be far more technologically advanced than us and would have nothing to fear from humans. So why would they only harass people on lonely roads or in the middle of the night? It would be no easy task to get here, so why come all this way to do nothing but buzz the locals?

Some people suggest the aliens are studying us, but if they wanted to do that why would they not just take a bunch of people from one place, similar to what we do when we study animals. After all, the aliens would most likely think of us in the same way. And since we couldn't stop them if we wanted to, they get a lot of people in one go.

Others propose the aliens don't make themselves known because they have something similar to Star Trek's Prime Directive, which bans interference with a primitive species. If that is the case, when they supposedly abduct people they aren't doing a very good job of observing without interfering.

And why are there so many different varieties of aliens and spacecraft designs? Given how difficult it is to get here, why send a different model of craft each time?

So, until someone provides indisputable proof of an extraterrestrial or their spacecraft, we need to remain healthily sceptical.

Getting a piece of the spacecraft might be a big ask, but these days everybody has a phone with a built-in camera, so by now someone should have taken a close-up photo. Admittedly it is possible to manufacture pictures through readily available software, but if you had seen an alien up close and taken a photo of it with your phone, surely you would at least offer it up for scrutiny and the chance to be the first person with irrefutable proof that extraterrestrials exist.

Lights in the sky are not proof of alien spacecraft either, no matter how many people see them. Lights could be anything and usually have natural explanations. Also, supposed memories retrieved by hypnosis are unreliable at best and don't constitute proof that the memory is correct.

Irrefutable proof would be aliens landing in the middle of the Sydney Cricket Ground in front of the world's media, stepping out and saying "Take me to your leader". Hopefully, they would then give public tours inside their craft, with me first in line.

I do not believe aliens visit the Earth. I do, however, believe there is life everywhere throughout the universe. I just don't think it has been here … yet.

I may not believe in alien visitations, but I do believe in UFOs. The acronym UFO stands for Unidentified Flying Object, although these days it is also common to see the acronym UAP, meaning Unidentified Aerial Phenomena. Therefore, anything in the sky you do not have an explanation for is a UFO. It does not mean there is no explanation for it, merely that you don't know what it is. I have looked at the sky almost continuously for 45 years and so far there are only 2 things I've seen that I couldn't explain at the time. However, at no moment did I ever think I was being buzzed by extraterrestrials, simply that I didn't immediately know what they were.

If UFOs aren't aliens, they must be something natural. Unfortunately, most people aren't familiar enough with astronomical objects, nor do they keep up to date with scientific events, well enough to identify the things they see. There are, however, some simple things you can do to help identify any flying object you do see and rather than immediately jumping to the conclusion it is an alien spacecraft, quite often the answer is not that hard to find.

Without a doubt, the most commonly mistaken object is Venus, but the following could also apply to Jupiter, Mars and some of the brighter stars.

Many people incorrectly believe that planets don't twinkle. This isn't true, especially if the planet is low on the horizon. Admittedly planets may not twinkle as much as stars, but they do twinkle. Twinkling is caused by the atmosphere, and the more turbulent the atmosphere, the more the stars and planets will twinkle. When a star or planet is low to the horizon, you are looking through more of the atmosphere and the twinkling can be particularly bad on some days. The other thing we need to know is that white light is made up of all the colours of the rainbow.

When you have something as bright as Venus low on the horizon, and it is a terrible evening for seeing, Venus will twinkle so much that it flashes through all the colours of the rainbow and appears to jiggle about furiously. This can catch people's attention. One night at work in Sydney I received an anxious phone call about a UFO with flashing lights that was flying around and making radical changes of direction. When the caller used binoculars, the object appeared even more unusual. The person was genuinely concerned and decided to call someone about it. After going through a list of questions, I looked out my office window and started to suspect it was Venus, which was sitting low on the western horizon at the time. Having an idea of what it might be, I described Venus to the caller and we both agreed it was, in fact, the planet he was observing. He hung up, feeling relieved and perhaps a little embarrassed that he had not recognised such an innocent object as Venus.

Another example of Venus misidentification involves seeing it during the daytime with your eyes. Now, the number of UFO reports that talk about people watching weather balloons or planes high up that suddenly see a UFO near the balloon/plane which then abruptly disappears sounds remarkably like an accidental Venus sighting. If the balloon/plane is high enough then, to see it, your eyes are effectively focussed at infinity. This is precisely what they have to do to see Venus. If the balloon/plane then happens to pass close by Venus' location, the observer will suddenly notice the bright planet. Look away, however, and your eyes defocus and Venus disappears, making it seem like the 'UFO' suddenly took off at great speed.

Sometimes a witness will describe how it circled the balloon. This sounds like a case of perspective producing the effect. If they are locked onto looking at the balloon, then it will appear centred and everything else will seem to move when in fact it may be the balloon moving around due to high altitude winds.

Other typical Venus UFO reports involve being chased for hours in the car.

Unlike a tree on the side of the road that appears to flash past as you drive down the highway, the further away an object is, the slower it seems to move past you. Now, even distant trees will eventually disappear out of view, but if you look at something off-world, say the Moon or Venus, you do not see them change position at all. They are always off to the side no matter how far you travel. It almost looks as if they are following you. I've often noticed this effect myself while travelling. Of course, they will slowly move, but this is due to the Earth's rotation rather than your driving skills.

Before you laugh, I have had to comment many times to Sydney news outlets on this exact thing in a professional capacity. The media would call for my opinion because they were going to run a story about a family that was followed from Canberra to Sydney by a UFO, or variations on this theme. One time I went to a TV station to look at the footage a family had filmed. As soon as I saw it, I knew it was Venus, and I told them so. That didn't stop them from running the story and somehow my explanation didn't make the cut.

That's not to say I don't make mistakes about UFOs. On one particular occasion, I had just finished a day at work where we had more than the usual number of calls about Venus. It was a Friday and immediately after work, I headed to Culburra, a small town on the coast just south of Sydney to spend the weekend with friends. That night we were walking along the beach when one of my friends asked me what a bright light was in the sky. I could see roughly where he was looking, so, without bothering to look up, I said it was Venus. It was sort of in the right direction. He then asked if I was sure. I said, yes. He said was I sure it wasn't a plane. I said, no, it was Venus, trust me. I still had not looked up at this stage. I had answered questions all day about Venus and I didn't want to go through the same routine with my friends. He pressed me and asked if I was positive it wasn't a plane, to which I replied, I know what I'm talking about. I wanted to change the subject. That ended the conversation until one minute later when the plane he had been looking at flew overhead on its way to the local airport. My friends still do not let me forget that night. Nor should they. For them, it was highly amusing, but I learnt a valuable lesson that night, always check something before you put your reputation on the line.

So far, I've talked about things I could explain. Is there anything I've seen that I can't explain? Yes, there are 2 things. Both occurred while I was out in Central Australia.

I was conducting a tour when what looked like a small bright cloud moved relatively quickly across the sky. It was a clear night with no other clouds and I surmised the lights of the resort were illuminating it, but the question remained why there was a small 'cloud' moving so quickly overhead and not dissipating. I still don't know.

The second event I can't explain looked like the headlights on a plane coming towards us. Nothing unusual there, as planes often have lights shining forward. But this light changed direction and moved away from us while the intensity of the light did not change. Had it been a forward-facing light on a plane, you would expect the light intensity to change. Also, there was no sound associated with it. The lack of sound could be explained if the aircraft was very high, but why the light didn't change is more perplexing. The next day we checked with the airport, and there was no local air traffic so we could discount that. It still, however, could have been a flight passing high over The Centre. I know what a satellite or meteor looks like and it wasn't one of those. To this day, I do not know what it was. My best guess is a plane, but who knows. At no time, however, did I think either of these events were alien spacecraft, only something I had no explanation for at the time.

Special events, such as the Sydney Olympics and the turn of the millennium, can also be particularly fruitful times for UFO sightings. I was working in Sydney during the 18 months leading up to the Olympics, and across the whole period there were special events and more than the usual number of sporting events. A lot of these employed spotlights and advertising blimps to draw attention to themselves. On cloudy nights, the spotlights would reflect off the bottom of the clouds as they moved around and reports of UFOs racing across the sky, making radical direction changes, would spike.

One annoying UFO was an internally illuminated advertising blimp. It was orange in colour and regularly hovered over sporting events. From a distance, it was impossible to see the advertising on its side, and it just looked like an orange, oval-shaped object stalking Sydney. When it was brought to our attention, we had a look through the telescope and immediately realised what it was. After a few sightings, whenever we saw the blimp in the sky, we would sigh inwardly and brace ourselves for the calls we knew would be coming our way.

Another UFO scare I had to decide on involved a mysterious light in the Sydney suburb of Manly. Two brothers that videoed it claimed it had followed them and that it kept changing shape. One of the TV news had picked up the story and wanted my thoughts to add to what they had filmed. As soon as I looked at it, I knew what it was. One thing that gave it away before I saw the footage was their statement that it followed them. To me, that meant it was probably the planet Venus, and once I saw the images, I knew it was. The continually changing shape they said were close-ups of the spacecraft was merely the autofocus on the poor camera trying to latch onto a point source in the sky. The video kept going in and out of focus and the distinct shape displayed when out of focus was simply the internal configuration of the camera. Once I was back at my office, I confirmed Venus would have been visible at the time and in the direction they described. The TV station played the story, with my comment included this time, but the brothers who filmed it still insisted it was an alien spacecraft.

Some people are just naturally predisposed to seeing UFOs as alien spacecraft. Anything they see that isn't obvious to them becomes extraterrestrial in origin, and nothing you say will ever change their minds. Throw in tiredness when driving on country roads, and it's not a big leap for people to transform everyday natural things into UFOs.

Many things foster reports of unknown flying objects. Apart from the above examples, other common possibilities (and this is by no means an exhaustive list) include auroras, sundogs, anomalous atmospheric refraction, weather balloons, reflections from fog and mist, headlights in the distance, eye defects, photo defects, and, of course, deliberate hoaxes.

Unknown does not mean alien. It merely means you don't know what it is, and the process of investigating provides opportunities to discover something new and potentially exciting about the world, and that is the best part of finding ourselves living in an amazing universe.

# Afterword

At last, we come to the end.

Hopefully, in the process of discovering these moments from my life, you have realised that even an average person has moments worth retelling. Individually they may not be exceptional, but collectively they show that I have done some remarkable things and experienced some moments that have shed light on my life and shown me it has been worth living. It doesn't completely solve my depression issue, but it has certainly helped smooth out the extreme aspects of the condition.

I do, however, have one final piece of advice. The main aspect I found that really helps is to be curious. Take interest in the universe around you and learn to enjoy the wonders it has to offer. Curiosity has been the key to bringing me back from the darker side of depression.

I can still remember during the years of the Apollo program, when I was between the ages of 8 and 12, watching the astronauts move about the surface of the Moon and wondering why they were bouncing and moving so slowly. Why couldn't they simply walk about normally? It was a simple observation that sparked a thought that ultimately led to my discovery of gravity. It's the simple things that often lead to the greatest realisation.

Similarly, a few years later I noticed something quite apparent that had eluded my attention up until that moment. We lived not too far from the beaches of Sydney, so during summer we frequently visited the ocean. I knew that the water in the Pacific Ocean was a deep blue colour but never gave it a thought why it was so until one day, while swimming in a friend's pool, the thought struck me that the water in the pool was clear. Why is water from the tap or in a swimming pool colourless yet the ocean was a beautiful blue colour? What was the difference? It took a few years of investigating, and several alternatives that ultimately turned out to be wrong, until I found the right reason while studying the physics of the atom and the nature of light at university.

The world has so many surprises that literally everything you study will give you pleasure, in both the journey and in eventually discovering the answer, and if you can find pleasure in the world around you it makes it harder for depression to take hold.

I wrote this book initially as a means to rediscover my own life and its meaning, but hopefully, it has given you the inspiration to do the same with your own and help you to appreciate that you too have led an interesting life.

My journey is far from over, and I have several items on my bucket list to do before I get to the end. You may like to create your own, and who knows, some of the ones below may appear on yours as well.

My bucket list (in order from 'must do' to 'would be nice if possible'):
1. See the total solar eclipse from my home in 2028 – this one really only requires patience and clear weather to achieve
2. See the planetary grouping in 2040 – again, this one only requires patience, longevity, and clear weather
3. Visit a few remaining towns of Australia with populations greater than 10,000 people. I have been to every town in the country with populations greater than 20,000, but a trip to western Victoria and southeast of Adelaide will see that list extended to every town with at least 10,000 people.
4. Cross the Simpson Desert again – this is one of my favourite places in the country and I really want to visit it again
5. See Lake Eyre up close while it is filled with water – even though

I have seen the lake with water, it was from a distance, and I have been up close to the lake, but it was dry at the time, so I want to see it up close with water and experience all the wildlife that comes with it

6. Visit Mt Connor – I have driven past many times and feel it is time to stop and explore this magnificent structure
7. Drive the Warburton Track across Western Australia from Uluru to Kalgoolie – this has to be the most remote drive you can do in the country so of course I have to experience it

I have a few overseas items, but that's only because what I want to see doesn't exist in Australia.

8. Visit Iceland to see auroras, a volcanic eruption, and glaciers
9. Visit the USA to go tornado chasing, tour the Kennedy Space Centre, see Yellowstone National Park before it blows up, and visit the observatories on the top of Moana Kea in Hawai'i (also so I can say I've stood at the top of the tallest mountain on Earth!)
10. *Maybe* visit Paris to get lost in the Louvre for a week


And remember, wonder can be found anywhere and everywhere you look in our vast universe, especially in your own life.

Moments in a Life

Moments in a Life

# Images

## PART ONE - CHRONOLOGY

### Chapter 1 – Growing up

Front veranda of my grandmother's house in Turramurra

Front of the house with a young Frangipani tree hiding the bedroom windows

Rear of my grandmother's house showing the outside toilet in the foreground right

The back veranda, repurposed by my grandmother after we had moved out

One year old me beside a very young Jacaranda tree in the back yard

My grandmother sitting on the front veranda, enjoying the sunshine and watching the world go by

The whole family clearing the block at Berowra

My grandmother and brother clearing the bush from the house block

The Berowra house starts taking shape

The almost finished house from the back. Note the laundry on the lower left and the height of the back of the house

The front of the almost completed house

The sandstone retaining walls and leveling of the back yard were all done by my father

The front of the Berowra house 25 years after it was built

Sandstone cave in the Pilliga region of NSW

View from the walk around the sandstone caves of the Pilliga forest

Moments in a Life

View from the walk around the sandstone caves of the Pilliga forest
The front of my parent's farm house in Northern NSW
The back and side of my parent's farm house in Northern NSW. Usually the spa was located on the concrete slab that now has the chairs and table
The view from my parent's farm house in Northern NSW
Me pretending I know what I'm doing when it comes to building a fence

## Chapter 2 - Education
Front page of a newspaper from the time of the Apollo 11 moon landing
A young me posing for an official Primary School photo
Hard at study for a university physics assignment

## Chapter 3 – Working life
Sydney Observatory
The Harbour Bridge, looking from between the two large domes at Sydney Observatory
Parkes Radiotelescope
Our portable planetarium, showing the inflated entrance way
The Macquarie University Observatory
Architectural design for the Orange Regional Conservatorium and Planetarium

## PART TWO - LIFE

## Chapter 4 – Injuries
Before surgery: X-ray of my lower spine showing how far the L5 vertebrae has slipped
After surgery: X-ray of my lower spine showing the titanium rods and screws

## Chapter 5 - Death
My grandmother, about a year before she died
My younger sister, a few months before she died
My father, 2 years before he died
My maternal great grandparents
My great great grandfather, great grandmother, grandmother and uncle
My mother and me, one month before she died

Moments in a Life

## Chapter 6 – Sport

Me, as a very young Australian Rules Football player

In the middle of the action playing Australian Rules Football

Murray River Canoe Marathon finish line, I am in the back of the far boat

White water rafting on the Nymboida River

Waterskiing on the Hawkesbury River

Sometimes ropes just break!

## Chapter 7 - Travelling

Volcano caldera on the Big Island of Hawai'i

Waikiki Beach on the island of O'ahu

Fisherman's Wharf in San Francisco, California

The Grand Canyon

A grove of redwood trees in Sequoia-Kings Canyon National Parks

The 'General Sherman' tree, the largest living thing on the planet (based on volume)

Yosemite Valley

Meteor (Barringer) Crater

Camping and canoeing weekend away, northwest of Sydney

Camping and bike riding weekend away, north of Sydney

Driving down a track in the Warrumbungle National Park, NSW

Barron Falls, west of Cairns, FNQ

Port Douglas beach from a nearby lookout

Crossing the Wenlock River, Cape York

An anthill on Cape York

The most northerly point on the Australian mainland

Creek crossing near Bamaga, Cape York

Beach at the tip of Cape York

The Gulf of Carpentaria at Karumba, QLD

Mount Isa, QLD

Queensland - Northern Territory border on the Barkley Tablelands

The town of Tibooburra, NSW

Monument to the explorers Burke and Wills at Cooper Creek, Innamincka QLD

Sign at the intersection of the Stuart Highway and Oodnadatta Track, South Australia

Hotel at William Creek, halfway along the Ooodnadatta Track

Lake Eyre South from a distance

Woomera, South Australia

Coober Pedy, South Australia

The Breakaways, South Australia

A Boab tree in the Kimberley region, Western Australia

Kununurra, Kimberley region, Western Australia

The Western Australia - Northern Territory boundary down the Tanami Track

The Bungle Bungles, Kimberley Region, Western Australia

Wolfe Creek Crater, down the Tanami Track from Halls Creek, Western Australia

Henbury Meteorite Crater, Northern Territory

Me, somewhere down the Tanami Track

Cable Beach, Broome, Western Australia

Iron ore being loaded onto a tanker, Port Hedland, Western Australia

Whale shark off Ningaloo Reef, Exmouth, Western Australia

Exmouth, Western Australia

Kalbarri Skywalk, Kalbarri National Park, Western Australia

Grove of Karri trees, Western Australia

Valley of the Giants Treetop Walk, Western Australia

Wave Rock, Western Australia

Hippos Mouth, Wave Rock National Park, Western Australia

90 Mile Straight, Nullabor, Western Australia

Storms over the Nullabor at Eucla, Western Australia

The Bunda Cliffs, Nullabor, South Australia

Katherine Gorge, Northern Territory

Katherine Gorge, Northern Territory

The Devils Marbles, Northern Territory

A single Devils Marble

Daly Waters Pub, Northern Territory

The Plenty Highway at Glenormiston, just inside the Queensland border

Sand dunes on the edge of the Simpson Desert

The start of the Birdsville Track at Marree, South Australia

The start of the Birdsville Track

The town of Birdsville, southwest Queensland

Alice Springs, Northern Territory

The Finke River, the oldest riverbed in the world

The Alice Springs camel farm

Kings Canyon, Northern Territory

Kings Creek at the bottom of Kings Canyon

Pool of water and associated snake at the end of Kings Creek

Mount Connor, Northern Territory

Uluru from a distance, Northern Territory

The base of the Uluru climb showing Chicken Rock (where people are grouped)

Moonrise over Uluru

Uluru

Kata Tjuta from a distance

Close up of some Kata Tjuta domes

Walking around Kata Tjuta

Moonrise over Kata Tjuta

Our temporary observatory set up in the resort's amphitheatre

Early morning flight over Uluru

Camels on the way to Lake Amadeus

Lake Amadeus

Radiotelescope dishes just outside Narrabri, New South Wales

Siding Spring Observatory, Warrumbungle National Park, New South Wales

The Anglo-Australian Telescope at Siding Spring Observatory

Thunderbolt's Cave

Hobart harbour, Tasmania

The Gordon River in southwestern Tasmania

The oldest stone span bridge in Australia, located in the town of Richmond, Tasmania

The rugged northwest corner of Tasmania

Cradle Mountain in the centre of Tasmania

Port Arthur ruins in southeastern Tasmania

## Chapter 8 – Interactions with the natural world

My sister and myself with our first, and only, pet rabbit

Getting to know the pigs on a relative's farm at Bellingen, NSW

One of the few friendly dogs I knew in my younger days

Playing with trout and lambs at a relative's fish farm near Dorrigo, NSW

Our family cat as a kitten

My mother's Blue Cattle Dog

My grandfather's Rosella that became a family pet after he died

Mum feeding the King Parrots

Lightning storm over Uluru

Water cascading off Uluru during a storm

A waterfall off Uluru

# PART THREE - PASSION

## Chapter 10 – Astronomy

My original copy of *Second Foundation* by Isaac Asimov

A proud owner and his first telescope

My first telescope now sits in the corner of the sunroom

The full moon (Image courtesy of Geoffrey Wyatt)

Features on the Moon (Image courtesy of Geoffrey Wyatt)

Earthshine on the moon (Image courtesy of Geoffrey Wyatt)

Lunar eclipse diagram

A partial lunar eclipse (Image courtesy of Geoffrey Wyatt)

A crescent Venus minutes before it passed in front of the sun (Image courtesy of Geoffrey Wyatt)

Jupiter and 3 moons (Image courtesy of Geoffrey Wyatt)

Saturn (Image courtesy of Geoffrey Wyatt)

A planetary conjunction in 2005

A planetary conjunction in 2011

Comet Shoemaker-Levy 9 viewing at Sydney Observatory

Omega Centauri, the best globular cluster in the sky (Image courtesy of James Baguley)

Centaurus A galaxy (Image courtesy of James Baguley)

The Large Magellanic Cloud galaxy

Solar eclipse diagram

A partial solar eclipse

Yulara and our observatory location

Our viewing platforms amongst the sand dunes

Our observatory with Uluru in the distance

Telescopes on the viewing deck

Observatory sign at the start of a track

The same sign now lives in my back yard

Waiting to be interviewed in the cold morning air

Being interviewed for a travel show

# About the Author

Rod Somerville is an author, newspaper columnist, radio presenter, guest speaker, walking astronomical encyclopaedia, and has suffered from depression for over half his life.

What began in an outer suburb of Sydney at the age of 10 as an obsession with science fiction, morphed into a life of showing the universe to anyone who would stop and listen. With degrees in Physics and Mathematics, Rod has worked as a science educator for over 40 years. He established and ran a public observatory at Uluru in Central Australia for several years and since returning to the east coast has been actively involved in the public education of science wherever he has gone.

He has never done anything of earth-shattering importance or fame, but, through retelling moments in his life, he came to the realisation that his stories are just as interesting and just as worthy of being told as those from anyone else. They have created an amazing, albeit unknown, life that helped him realise living with depression isn't all bad.

# One Star by Day, Six Thousand by Night

## Discovering the Universe

Have you ever wanted to explore the night sky but didn't know how to get started?

Discovering the universe can be a daunting hobby when you first begin. Finding out what you need and how you go about observing the cosmos is not immediately obvious.

Through a career spanning 45 years as a science communicator, Rod Somerville takes you on a journey that bridges the gap between being a complete novice to that of a keen amateur astronomer. Offering inspiration, insight, and information in easy to understand language, he makes the universe accessible to everyone. Along the way you will discover answers to almost every question a budding astronomer might ask – and more.

Parents will value this book as a resource, enabling them to answer all those pesky questions from children, or grandchildren, wanting to acquire a telescope or binoculars for Christmas. And what do you do if you see a UFO? With many thoughts not found in any other astronomy book, it is a must read before immediately jumping to an extra-terrestrial conclusion.

If you ever find yourself looking at the stars and wanting to discover more about the universe, then this is the book for you.

www.ingramcontent.com/pod-product-compliance
Lightning Source LLC
Chambersburg PA
CBHW051421290426
44109CB00016B/1379